The
Interactive
Corporation

The
Interactive
Corporation

Using Interactive Media and Intranets
to Enhance Business Performance

Roger Fetterman

Sponsored by Apple Computer, Inc.
Apple Developer Relations Group
for the Apple Media Program

New York Toronto London Sydney Auckland

The Interactive Corporation

Copyright © 1997 by Roger Fetterman

Published in the United States by Random House, Inc., New York and simultaneously in Canada by Random House of Canada, Limited.

Library of Congress Cataloging-in-Publication Data
Fetterman, Roger L.
    The interactive corporation: using interactive media and intranets to enhance business performance / by Roger Fetterman.
    p. cm.
    Includes index.
    ISBN 0-375-40092-3
    1. Multimedia systems in management. 2. Interactive multimedia. I. Title.
HD30.212.F47 1997
658'.0567--dc20   97-22978
                                 CIP

Publisher	Charles Levine
Development Editor	Jennifer Dowling
Production Editor	Joseph Vella
Cover Design	Electrik Graffiti, New York, New York
Interior Design	VersaTech Associates, San Diego, California
Page Composition	Sybil Ihrig, VersaTech Associates
Proofreader	Deborah O. Stockton

Typeset and printed in the United States of America.

Visit the Random House Web site at http://www.randomhouse.com/

This book is available for special purchases in bulk by organizations and institutions, not for resale, at special discounts. Please direct your inquiries to the Random House Special Sales Department, toll-free 888-591-1200 or fax 212-572-4961.

Please address inquiries about electronic licensing of this division's products, for use on a network or in software or on CD-ROM, to the Subsidiary Rights Department, Random House Reference & Information Publishing, fax 212-940-7370/

First Edition
0 9 8 7 6 5 4 3 2 1
ISBN: 0-375-40092-3

New York Toronto London Sydney Auckland

Outline

Contents

4 Planning and Analysis—The Basis for Success 97

5 Interactive Media in Distribution 131

6   Interactive Media in Manufacturing 191

7   Interactive Media in Finance
    and Human Resources 235

Preface

Methodologies for determining how best to apply technology to business processes are not new. In the early 1980s, while I was working for Bell Northern Research (BNR), a wholly owned subsidiary of Northern Telecom (now Nortel) and Bell Canada, I worked in an internal start-up group called Project Launch. The objective of the group was to take a new product concept, based on the integration of computer and communications technologies, to market. During the course of our primary market research, we had the opportunity to develop a thorough understanding of the business processes in the reinsurance industry.

Our objective was to trial a product that was the first example of the use of computer-telephony integration or CTI technology. CTI allows a computer to receive information from telephone switching equipment and initiate appropriate actions that take advantage of the capabilities of both the computer and the switch. For example, if calling party ID information was available, the switch could send the phone number of the calling party to the computer. An application program could open a file related to the phone number and automatically present the information on the screen of a workstation or personal computer.

In a customer service environment, a customer call would trigger retrieval of relevant records. As a result, the party answering the call would have up-to-date information about the account at his or her fingertips and be able to respond appropriately to the caller. If the customer service agent determines that a particular individual or group is best equipped to respond to the customer, the calling party and the corresponding computer file would be simultaneously transferred to the individual or group.

The Project Launch team was able to convince the reinsurance group of Continental Insurance to trial the Gemini system. Our prime contact at Continental was senior manager Jim Hynes. Fortunately, Jim had the ability to recognize the potential value of a technology to business processes. As I was later to discover, not everyone was able to link that value of the system to his or her business operation as easily as Jim had done. After our first meeting, all of us were excited by the prospects for success.

Notwithstanding our excitement about the opportunity, our team needed to prove that the Gemini system, which consisted of a small computer and a small switch that were logically and physically connected by a command and status link, was a valid solution. The system was intended for small businesses with up to 15 users. Members of our team began to flow chart the entire process at one of Continental's reinsurance offices.

Reinsurance companies provide insurance for huge building complexes, such as the World Trade Center in New York. Individual insurers are loath to accept all of the risk associated with such a facility, so reinsurance companies develop an insurance package that is backed by a few dozen individual insurers. Both risk and reward are shared.

Whenever any change in the coverage is requested by customers, the reinsurance company must go back to the insurers to inform them of the change and its impact and to determine if they will continue to participate—and, if so, at what level. Thus the reinsurance agent had to review the existing deal with each insurer, calculate the impact of the change, and relay the information to each insurer.

When an insurer called into Continental, the company wanted to be able to pull up the relevant file instantly, so the business discussion could proceed posthaste. This was difficult to accomplish using a paper-based process to handle dozens of properties and hundreds of insurers.

Our team worked with the reinsurance office in Philadelphia to complete the flow chart. We examined all of the activities, determined which could be enhanced through the use of the Gemini system, and estimated the potential impact of the system. In our report, we told our customers at Continental that the Gemini system could save them 30 percent on each reinsurance transaction. We were nonplused when they told us that we were wrong, but delighted when they said that their calculations showed that the savings were more like 70 percent.

My experience with the remarkable individuals at Continental Insurance and BNR taught me a valuable lesson. A detailed understanding of business processes can help both buyers and sellers to understand and establish measurable benefits from the application of technology. When I proposed this book to Random House and Apple Computer, I knew that the methodology we had used in the early 1980s would be valuable for applying networked interactive media capabilities to core business processes.

During my search for success stories and case studies for this book, I talked to many individual corporate users, developers, and consultants in the interactive media marketplace. Some of them remarked that the methodology I advocate for applying technology in businesses—based on a thorough understanding of business processes—is not new. It has existed for several decades. However, they all agreed that it is not being applied in businesses.

As I continued to gather information about the successes enjoyed by businesses, it became clear that the process works, and it works well. As you read this book, you'll note that many companies have successfully applied interactive media to their business processes. While it is gratifying to note that the methodology works, it is not clear why it is used so infrequently by companies.

For the moment, it is enough that this book provides the framework and many examples of the successful application of interactive media in business environments.

Acknowledgments

Books such as this one can never be written by an individual in isolation. Many people are involved, some of whom I've never met in person. We've talked on the phone, exchanged e-mail messages, and sometimes traded books. It has been immensely gratifying to find kindred spirits who are willing to help, sight unseen, in the never-ending search for more information. Many thanks to all of you who helped with this book.

Thanks to all of the kind souls from AlliedSignal, Apple Computer, Bandag, Booz•Allen & Hamilton, California State Automobile Association, DiaCom Technologies, the Dublin Group, General Machinery, International Data Corporation, Ikonic Interactive, McDonnell Douglas Helicopter, Nortel, RDC Interactive, Reuters NewMedia, Robertson Associates, and other companies who helped me flesh out the case studies and success stories.

There are a number of special people who provided advice and encouragement and precious contacts in areas that I needed to visit. Chris Okon gave me an opportunity to prepare a chapter in *New Media Market Trends* in 1995 and encouraged me to submit my proposal for this book to Random House and Apple Computer. She also introduced me to Dana De Puy Morgan of Apple Computer, who has enthusiastically supported the concept and development of the book. Dana provided ideas, contacts, and editorial support and suggested case studies. Lisa Wellman (formerly of Apple Computer) has supported my efforts to produce the book ever since I first met her at the Apple New Media Forum in June 1995. Susan Lawson and Charles Levine of Random House provided advice and encouragement and helped in numerous ways to make this a better book.

My faithful friend and expert reviewer, Randall Seger, challenged and extended my thinking and helped me get back on track when I was lost. In addition, he provided many useful insights to make the message clearer and the book more valuable to the reader. I thank him for reviewing the manuscript at several stages in its development.

As usual, my family supported my efforts. Cynthia Mitchell and Bill Youngman introduced me to some fruitful avenues in the advertising and manufacturing processes, for which I am grateful.

Finally I thank my wife Lynn for being patient and steadfast in her support. This book is dedicated to her.

Roger L. Fetterman

Introduction

Over the past decade, the industrialized world has embraced the "digitization" of each of the principal forms of media used for mass communications. Text, graphics, animation, photographic images, audio, and video are all readily available in digital form.

Terms such as "multimedia," "digital revolution," and "digital convergence" litter our information landscape. Each of these terms has been subjected to so much hyperbole in marketing proclamations that the potential business value of digital media is often obscured.

All of the above terms suffer from the same shortcoming: "What do they mean?" The definition is often a source of confusion because there is no consensus among the constituents. The term "multimedia" means different things to different people—everything from CD-ROMs to special effects in television programming and movies to interactive learning systems and electronic catalogs. However, the "meaning" that is important is: "What does it mean to me and my business?"

I wrote this book specifically to address the latter "meaningful question" because digital media have the potential to transform the world of business, as well as that of education, entertainment, and government. This is true because any and all of the digital media can be mediated by personal computers so they are truly *interactive* media.

When information and knowledge are in interactive media form, they can be specifically tailored to the performance, learning, and communication needs of individuals and groups in business. Time and distance obstacles are overcome because interactive media can be available when and where needed by individuals and groups. This enables individuals and groups to conference and collaborate on demand.

In this increasingly competitive global marketplace, most companies continuously scan the horizon for solutions that increase organizational effectiveness. Interactive media enable organizations to "extract" the "hidden gold" of their intellectual assets and deploy them appropriately to contribute to the overall good of the organization and its employees.

Many organizations have proven that interactive media solutions provide a highly effective vehicle for enhancing organizational communications and business processes. Investments in interactive media solutions typically generate higher rates of return than are found for technology investments. The success stories and case studies in this book demonstrate that the appropriate application of interactive media often helps companies achieve breakthrough results.

As used in this book, the term "interactive" means a bi-directional input/feedback process between a human being and preprogrammed digital content. I intend to use the term "interactive media" rather than "multimedia" for most of the success stories and case studies in this book. Even though multimedia was the starting point for the research and analysis that is the foundation of this book, "interactive media" will be used in almost all situations.

Even when "multimedia" seems to be clearly defined (Figure I–1), the definition doesn't help us understand where, how, when, or if multimedia can be used advantageously in a business setting. Sometimes the term results in controversy about whether a particular application is indeed a "multimedia application." I have often been told that a particular application was not really "multimedia" because it did not include audio and video.

Multimedia is defined as a set of digital capabilities that support the use of audio, photo-realistic images, and video—in addition to text, graphics, and animation—for enhancing the communication of information and the transfer of knowledge. The richness of an information conduit is enhanced when users can *interact* with the digitized content, whether it consists of static media such as text and graphics or dynamic media such as audio and video.

Multimedia-based computing consists of up to six digital data types of interactive media—text, graphics, animation, audio, images, and video (Figure I–1). This applies to stand-alone applications used by a single user as well as net-worked applications used collaboratively by multiple individuals or groups.

No single media type is inherently better than another. Each has its own strength in communications and should be

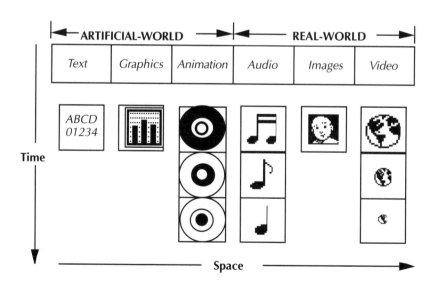

Figure I–1. The addition of real-world media (i.e., audio, images, and video) adds a new dimension to the effectiveness of computer-mediated business communications.
Source: Authenticity

employed accordingly (for example, text is excellent for presenting factual data, while audio is excellent for eliciting or conveying emotion, etc.).

Interactive media allow us to focus on the use of available digitized media in the context of the business environment in question. Our primary concern is not with the merits of media types but with the value of interactive media in business processes.

> *If multimedia has become the thread, then interactive media is becoming the fabric for effective communication of information and transfer of knowledge in business.*

All of the technologies needed are available today to implement mission-critical business solutions based on interactive media. This book describes how the reader can make a direct correlation between interactive media and the need to increase profitability, improve products, enhance customer service, improve velocity to market, and contain costs. Businesses that understand the value of information and corporate know-how, delivered to individuals and teams in the context of business processes, will appreciate the framework, methodologies, and tools contained herein.

A business process is a series of related tasks or activities designed to effect a measurable goal. Your corporation must thoroughly understand and indoctrinate itself in its business processes to achieve the kind of breakthroughs and successes profiled in this book. Four core business processes will be discussed:

- ❑ Distribution (which includes marketing, sales, customer service, and distribution and warehousing)
- ❑ Finance
- ❑ Human Resources
- ❑ Manufacturing (which includes research and development, product design, and production)

Many best-selling business book authors advocate the transformation of organizations into self-managing, multidisciplinary teams. Such teams are revolutionizing the economics of business by enabling their organizations to respond to the fast-moving changes taking place in the global economy. This prospect is challenging and exciting and totally necessary if organizations are to thrive in the next millennium. The thesis of this book is that networked interactive media can help transform the business organization into one that can successfully compete in today's and tomorrow's global marketplace.

Interactive media can enable individuals and groups to share, annotate, and manipulate information at their desktops in real time, regardless of where they are located. It can provide the intimate and rich communications environments needed to share important information and knowledge and to make the decisions necessary to fulfill corporate objectives. It can help companies realize the payoffs (Figure I–2).

Team members need to be trained to ensure they can function effectively in new ways in their new roles. Interactive media may provide the perfect means for making possible this transformation. It may be the best vehicle for communicating information and transferring knowledge in these new organizational structures.

Whether we use the term "multimedia" or "interactive media," executives know what they want and need: effective

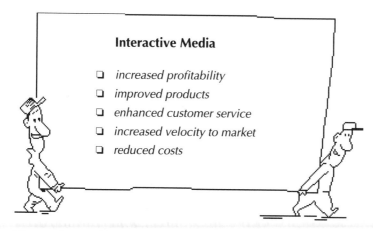

Figure I–2. The payoffs of using interactive media in business processes

solutions that enhance the operation of their businesses. Business people need to understand how interactive media capabilities can be used to better respond to new business opportunities and to meet competitive threats. Why should executives be interested in interactive media unless the value can be shown in the context of the day-to-day business operations?

Interactive media, particularly as related to private networks or intranets, are being applied in the context of business processes. Corporations that are fully cognizant of their core business processes are in the enviable position of being able to deploy a technological infrastructure as an asset to support improvements in those processes.

This book is organized so that readers can go through it according to their specific interests and understanding of the subject matter. If customer service is your passion, start with Chapter 5. If you want to delve into some of the reasons that businesses have struggled to make interactive media work for them, go to Chapter 1, and so on. Above all else, please enjoy this book.

Corporations for the New Millennium   Chapter 1 reviews the threats and opportunities that corporations face as they move toward the new millennium. The business/interactive media gap that exists between the constituents is explored, as are the gaps between business and information technology groups. The chapter closes with recommendations for closing the gaps.

Traditional and Emerging Uses of Interactive Media in Business   Chapter 2 reviews traditional interactive media applications and comments on emerging interactive media solutions. Following a discussion of the value of the Internet and other technologies, I explore performance support solutions that provide new levels of adaptability.

Interactive Media Roles in Today's and Tomorrow's Business   Chapter 3 begins the discussion of the role that interactive media can and should play in business. Following a review of the different roles we play as customers of interactive media technologies, I introduce a useful way of looking at interactive media solutions as four different application types. The chapter concludes with case studies that map into the application types. From modest beginnings as content-centric applications, Apple's Service Source and Lam Research's Interactive Maintenance System are becoming excellent examples of performance support solutions.

Planning and Analysis—The Basis for Success   Chapter 4 introduces the reader to the planning process for interactive media projects that the author highly recommends for use in all business processes. Each step in the planning process is discussed in detail. The chapter concludes with a case study based on the successful sales automation efforts of Hewlett-Packard's Computer Systems Organization.

Interactive Media in Distribution   Chapter 5 explores each of the distribution processes. It suggests that integrated solutions should be developed since each of the constituent processes is customer-centric. Case studies and success stories follow a discussion of the individual processes that make up the distribution process. Significant return-on-investment opportunities await those who apply themselves in this area.

Interactive Media in Manufacturing   Chapter 6 describes the constituent processes in the manufacturing process. Interactive media solutions range from interactive media assembly instructions to collaborative computing and conferencing with customers and external suppliers during the product development process. This chapter includes case studies for companies that "manufacture" intellectual assets as their fundamental business operation, as well as more traditional manufacturing operations. The results of interactive media investments range from improved product quality to breakthroughs in performance.

Interactive Media in Finance and Human Resources   Chapter 7 reveals more about the potential that exists for interactive media in the finance and human resources processes than it does about success stories. It covers investments by human resource organizations in intranet and kiosk technology as a means of providing "self-service" to employees. I postulate that both core processes have opportunities for leveraging interactive media, but the processes may need to change so they match up with the fundamental structural changes that are occurring in many businesses.

Summary and Conclusions   Chapter 8 provides a brief review of the opportunities that are available in each of the core business processes. It also looks at a conundrum: "Why don't all companies invest in interactive media given that many organizations have achieved outstanding results?" I conclude that many companies are not equipped with the resources and tools needed to realize the benefits inherent in interactive media solutions that map into their business processes. This book was written to help companies take full advantage of the latent opportunities available to those who understand their business processes.

This book provides the framework and tools needed by decision makers to apply interactive media to core business processes in line with corporate goals and objectives. It recognizes an evolutionary trend from standalone applications to performance support solutions and networked interactive media solutions.

There is a hierarchical structure associated with this evolution that makes it evident that interactive media solutions are being deployed in different ways with corresponding differences in the impact they have on corporations. It extends from the application of interactive media in traditional applications to networked solutions in core business processes:

1. Computer-based training or business presentations. When the use of the tool is complete, it is put to one side and employees get on with their jobs. Both are standalone applications that may be more cost effective than other ways to realize the same outcome.

Neither is part of an overall effort to enhance a particular business process.

2. Performance support systems, directed toward several of the tasks or activities of an individual rather than toward the entire process. An example may be a sales support system using an interactive media product catalog that has modules for creating customized presentations and product and service proposals. Such systems can be invaluable to sales representatives in the field. These systems are extensible to solutions that satisfy the entire business process.

3. Performance solutions directed specifically toward business processes. They can address relevant activities and tasks of the individuals and groups involved and allow them to collaborate in a specific area of business. As discussed later in this book, interactive media are invaluable for performance solutions in all of the distribution and manufacturing processes and hold great promise in finance and human resources. By addressing individual activities and tasks and also allowing player access to appropriate knowledge bases, individuals and groups can collaborate and function as effective multidisciplinary teams. These solutions are directed toward business operations.

This evolving structure is in sync with the needs of corporations that are preparing for the new millennium. Performance support systems recognize that an organization's human resources are its most important asset, and that networked interactive media can satisfy the communications, performance, and training needs of employees.

1

Corporations for the New Millennium

In the first half of this decade we witnessed a good deal of commotion because of the application and misapplication of business practices such as reengineering. For many employees, corporate downsizing forced career changes that might never have been considered otherwise. For some companies, it meant changes to the fundamental ways that business would be conducted. In spite of the trauma experienced by individuals and corporations, a profound transformation took place in the way that all of us regarded information and knowledge.

Information and knowledge have become the currency of a new economy because they are being made available to employees whenever and wherever they are needed through the technologies developed to support the Internet and the World Wide Web. The explosive growth in intranet deployment by businesses is evidence of corporate commitment to delivering information and knowledge to employees.

As a result, interactive media assume more value than ever before, since this may be the most effective mechanism we have for delivering information and transferring knowledge.

Corporate Imperatives and Business Processes

In the 1990s, the following corporate imperatives emerged as critical to the prosperity (and in some cases, the survival) of corporations in the emerging global marketplace:

- ❏ Rapid response to opportunities or threats
- ❏ Increased velocity to market for products
- ❏ Development and delivery of value-added products
- ❏ Achievement and maintenance of a technological advantage
- ❏ Delivery of more robust customer service and support

All projects, including interactive media proposals, must be evaluated to determine their contribution to these corporate goals (see Figures 1–1 and 1–2). For instance, will the proposed sales automation system help the company launch a new product more rapidly and successfully? Can a performance support system help product management develop value-added products that match specialized customer needs? Will an interactive, media-based customer response system make your company an industry leader in service and support? Can the just-in-time training and reference system help factory floor workers build products that are better customized for individuals? Will electronic service manuals with interactive diagnostic capabilities significantly improve maintenance services?

In some cases, interactive media applications will meet more than one of these overall goals. When interactive media capabilities are deployed to satisfy both corporate imperatives and the goals of core business processes, the applications are likely to be resoundingly successful. And the payback will definitely show on the bottom line.

Interactive media capabilities can be used either as an *offensive* weapon to gain advantage over competitors or as a *defensive* response to catch up to the competition. For example,

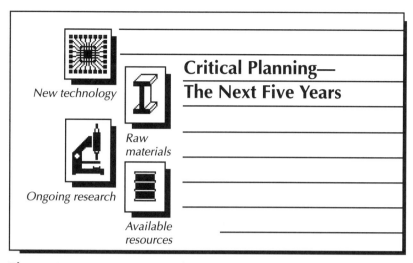

Figure 1–1. Interactive media must be included in current five-year plans.

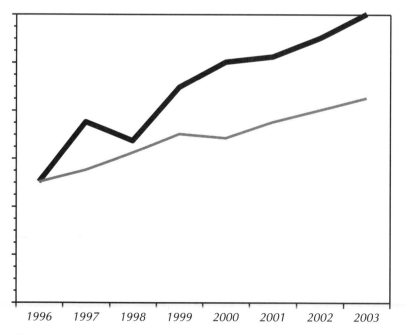

Figure 1–2. Interactive media can impact the bottom line.

production cycles can be reduced by introducing just-in-time training in a factory to acquaint employees with new assembly procedures and to certify that employees have achieved the required level of competency before using the new procedures. The first company to use interactive media in this fashion achieves an offensive competitive advantage. Its competitors are then forced to respond defensively—either by replicating the interactive media project or by taking some other action.

Changing Information Needs

All businesses seem to be in the position in which they must make everything happen faster. Product life cycles for complex products have gone from years to months. Today's state-of-the-art products can be obsolete tomorrow. In this faster-paced environment, decisions must be made in real time, which means that instantaneous access to information, knowledge, and co-workers must be available. The information infrastructure of the corporation must change to support the "real-time" nature of today's business operations.

In the past, preservation of legacy computer and communications systems was a tenet of good business management. Now it has the potential to become a millstone around the neck of the corporation. The information infrastructure must now change to reflect the "run rate" of business processes. Choices based on cost avoidance can lead to bad decisions in an environment where the fundamental processes of the organization must accelerate to match the need for more speed.

Adapting to a Changing Workplace

Organizations that have not adapted quickly to changes in the business environment have suffered dramatic declines. Witness the drop in market share of computer industry leaders such as International Business Machines and Digital Equipment Corporation. At the same time, other computer businesses like Hewlett-Packard and Microsoft have enjoyed rapid growth because they adjusted their operations to suit current societal, business, and technological shifts.

Reengineering demonstrated how to integrate functionally separated tasks into unified, horizontal work processes. *Reengineering the Corporation* (Champy and Hammer, 1993) helped define one of the most influential management concepts to emerge in years. Reengineering inspired executives and managers to rethink and redesign basic business processes, such as customer service, order fulfillment, and product development. Some companies realized significant improvements in productivity, customer satisfaction, and quality while significantly cutting costs.

However, in many instances, reengineered processes fell far short of their goals. The promised improvements were never realized. Reengineering sometimes simply became another way to downsize the organization. Champy (1995) concluded that the key problem is management itself. Business operations cannot be reengineered without changing the way managers think as well as how they do their jobs.

For example, in *Interactive Selling in the '90s*, a book I co-authored, we noted that success in sales (process) automation depends on:

- ❏ Securing the cooperation of the sales force
- ❏ Establishing measurable business and sales goals
- ❏ Modeling the business process or processes in question
- ❏ Demonstrating success through pilot programs
- ❏ Establishing a support infrastructure

Only by addressing *all* of these issues could one change the way sales management and the rank-and-file conduct business (Fetterman and Byrne, 1995).

Champy's *Reengineering Management* (1995) advises the reader to "organize, inspire, deploy, enable, measure, and reward the value-adding operational work." This book is based on the belief that technology can and should be applied to business processes such that it satisfies not only the needs of the individual performing the tasks but also the goals of the business.

In recent years, business managers have started to notice that horizontal processes, those that cut across divisional and departmental boundaries, are important to the success of the corporation (Ghoshal and Bartlett, 1995). Total quality management cuts across organizations to instill quality in the company's products and services.

The research by Ghoshal and Bartlett was based on 20 companies in Japan, the United States, and Europe whose top management recognized that business processes are more important than organizational structure. In these companies, the core processes that cut across the organization chart were more important than the vertical, authority-based hierarchical structure.

As a first step, these companies enhanced creativity and promoted entrepreneurship in front-line managers. A second process built competence across the company's organizational boundaries. And, finally, a third process promoted continuous renewal of the strategies and ideas that drove the business. So, according to Ghoshal and Bartlett, three core organizational processes exist in a healthy corporation: the entrepreneurial process, the competence-building process, and the renewal process.

Managerial support of these core organizational processes is also important to the success of introducing interactive media in business, since managers recognize:

❑ The value of the individual
❑ The need to develop the overall competency of the organization
❑ The importance of converting data into information and information into knowledge.

Closing the Business/Interactive Media Gap

Business executives are more likely to understand the value of interactive media when it is directly related to business processes. This firmly places the interactive media proposal in the context of management thinking, since it can be related directly to corporate and process goals. Interactive media applications that are justified solely on the basis of potential cost savings may have limited perceived value on the overall operation of an enterprise. This suggests that the interactive media community needs to shift its perspective and put interactive media solutions in a business context. The context may change for different types of businesses, but the fundamental premise remains the same: interactive media solutions must be positive factors in satisfying corporate goals and objectives.

Business/Information Technology Gap

The gap between the business and information technology groups in business has been documented by a number of organizational leaders. Charles B. Wang, CEO of Computer Associates International, Inc., defines the gap or *disconnect* as:

> The Disconnect: A *conflict, pervasive yet unnatural, that has misaligned the objectives of business managers and technologists and that impairs or prevents organizations from obtaining a cost-effective return on their investment in information technology.*
>
> —Wang, 1994

In the 1980s, information technologists built systems that were justified on the basis of labor reduction. Most of these relatively easy opportunities to automate have been carried out in manufacturing environments. However, in some cases it was difficult to determine if the promise of the technology was actually delivered.

In spite of huge investments, business productivity did not rise as expected, and many American businesses moved manufacturing facilities offshore. Jobs were lost to foreign competitors in almost direct proportion to the loss of market share. Cost reduction based on labor displacement may not have been the most appropriate goal for the times.

Technology alone is not to blame. Although there were many instances in which the technology did not live up to its promises—perhaps the hardware and software were late or too difficult to use—the real problem remained and continues to remain the same: matching technological capabilities with business goals. CEOs and direct reports must be able to articulate the company's goals so that information technologists can respond accordingly. Information technologists, in turn, must be able to articulate how new technologies can contribute to meeting corporate goals.

The challenge in the new millennium is to determine how to get measurable value through investments in new computer and communications technologies and digitized content. Information technologists must be able to incorporate and integrate new technologies in business processes to increase profitability, improve service, improve competitive advantage, and increase revenue.

Business/Interactive Media Gap

Although interactive media is in its second decade, there are as yet no trade shows or conferences dedicated to interactive media business applications. Most shows and conferences focus on the technology, the tools, and the interactive media developer community. As a result, there is little to attract business and information technology managers. And yet, if management does not understand what interactive media mean in a business context, then interactive media will appear to have limited value in business.

To my knowledge, there seems to be only one book that discusses the general application of multimedia in business: *Mainstream Multimedia*, which I co-authored with Satish Gupta in 1993. Dozens of books provide "how-to" information and cover the intricacies of the technologies needed to implement multimedia applications. These books are invaluable to the development community but have little value to business and information technology managers who want to take advantage of interactive media solutions. I believe that this is the first book that relates interactive media to business processes.

In the main, the use of interactive media capabilities has been confined to training and business presentations. Interactive media have come into vogue because of the rapid growth in the use of the Internet, the Web, and intranets in business environments. However, the developer communities have not established links between interactive media capabilities and business process needs. By establishing direct correlation between interactive media and the need to (1) increase profitability, (2) improve customer service, (3) improve the velocity to market, and (4) contain costs, the interactive media and business communities can establish a common framework for working together (see Table 1–1).

The appropriate application of interactive media capabilities to business processes can ensure that corporate goals are met and, in some cases, provide breakthroughs in performance. Corresponding results are difficult to achieve with standalone applications since the use of interactive media cannot be related directly to the overall operation of the business. For example, standalone computer-based training may be less costly than traditional lecture/lab training, but how can its value be connected to an overall corporate goal such as "improving customer service?" If the course material becomes part of a performance support system, the impact of just-in-time learning can be ascertained using the measures established for the customer service process. Recent improvements in computer and networking technologies enable organizations to take advantage of the rich communications environment that networked interactive media make manifest.

Application	Type	How Justified	Corporate Goals
Computer-based training	Standalone	Less expensive than lecture/lab Better retention by students	No direct link to corporate goals
Business presentations	Standalone	More impact than traditional methods	No direct link to corporate goals
Performance support system for sales	Sales process	Increased profitability Reduced selling costs Improved customer service	Results are aligned with corporate goals
Interactive media work instructions for assembly technicians	Production process	Reduced manufacturing cycle times Improved product quality	Results are aligned with corporate goals

Table 1–1. Comparison between standalone and business process-centric application of interactive media capabilities

Technology Explosions

We are witnessing an incredible explosion in new technologies that makes it more and more difficult to understand, evaluate, and deploy computer and communications equipment. Vendors find it more difficult to introduce new technologies to business and information technology managers in ways that allow them to see how the use of the technology will be advantageous to their business.

Today, interactive media computers[1] are the norm. Vendors offer a wide range of such computers to all segments of the market, including home offices and consumers in addition to businesses.

The advent of interactive-media notebook computers as powerful as desktop units, especially combined with

Figure 1–3. Notebook computers have enabled the use of interactive media in field sales and service applications.

enhanced communications such as high-speed modems and cellular data, allows field personnel to take advantage of interactive media solutions. Notebook computers (see Figure 1–3) have become the playback unit for interactive media presentations and learning modules and the personal communicator of the sales representative. Field service personnel use notebook computers to access hypermedia maintenance manuals that contain assembly drawings and information, maintenance and diagnostic procedures, and product upgrade information. Animation, photo-realistic images, and video are utilized advantageously throughout these electronic documents.

Although the mainframe computer has not gone away, the availability of powerful, high-capacity servers has enabled the creation of the client/server paradigm. Client/servers enable businesses to deliver information and knowledge to employees where, when, and how they need them.

Interactive media servers are being made available by all of the major players, including Hewlett-Packard, IBM, Silicon Graphics, and Sun Microsystems, in addition to Apple Computer.

Advances in networking technology have enabled Ethernet and token ring to support interactive applications.

Both LAN types are available in switched versions which provide dedicated 10 Mbps (million bits per second) and 16 Mbps bandwidth to individual desktops.

Two competing Fast Ethernet schemes which emerged in 1992 have become standards. Both extend the bandwidth of Ethernet to 100 Mbps. Fast Ethernet, which is very similar to the original Ethernet standard, delivers 100 Mbps on shared media. Likewise, 100VG-AnyLAN delivers 100 Mbps but it uses a hub-based switching system. Both are capable of supporting time-sensitive traffic such as audio and video to desktop users.

Asynchronous Transfer Mode (ATM) technology is moving from the network backbone to the desktop, offering 25.6 Mbps or 155 Mbps to the desktop. ATM promises to enable the deployment of a network in the future that will be capable of integrating data, video, and voice at bandwidths as high as 622 Mbps. At this point, businesses can choose from several different networking technologies to interconnect interactive media users (see Table 1–2). Switched technologies are generally preferred for applications that use time-based media because the available bandwidth can be dedicated to individual users.

In August 1995, Starlight Networks and Sun Microsystems teamed up to introduce a bundled, video-based Training on Demand (TOD) solution that uses an interactive media network to deliver interactive, computer-based training to users at their desktops. TOD is based on Starlight's StarWorks®

Technology	Shared or Switched	Bandwidth (Mbps)
Ethernet	Shared or switched	10
Token Ring	Shared or switched	16
Fast Ethernet	Shared	100
100VG-AnyLAN	Switched	100
Asynchronous Transfer Mode	Switched	26.5, 155, and 622

Table 1–2. Characteristics of technologies for networked interactive media

interactive media networking software and Sun Micro-systems' SPARC-based servers and courses from J3 Learning and ITC.

Remote access technology for field personnel is still an impediment for personnel in the field. Even the fastest modems and basic rate ISDN are not practical for transport-ing large interactive media files over the network. An interac-tive media product catalog could easily be several hundred megabytes or even a few gigabytes in size. As shown in Table 1–3, it takes a relatively long time to download a 10 MB file even when using ISDN. Broadband networks, at 1.544 Mbps or more, begin to offer reasonable transport times.

Historically, networks and servers have adhered to the 80/20 rule. In this scenario, 80 percent of the traffic generated on a network segment is local and 20 percent is routed to the wide area network (WAN) or the Internet. This applies to both voice and data traffic. However, recent shifts to flatter organi-zations and self-managing teams have changed the flow of information in many corporations. Modern desktop comput-ing technologies and the ubiquitous connectivity provided by the Internet and intranets are changing this rule. In fact, most of the traffic generated may be for WANs or the Inter-net. This prompts the need for high-performance backbone

Network/Speed	Transfer Time
PSTN/9.6 kbps modem	2.3 hours
PSTN/14.4 kbps modem	1.5 hours
PSTN/28.8 kbps modem	46 minutes
Switched 56 kbps/56 kbps modem	24 minutes
Basic Rate ISDN (128 kbps)	10 minutes
Switched T1 connection (1.544 Mbps)	52 seconds
10 Mbps cable modem	8 seconds
ATM 155 Mbps	0.5 seconds

PSTN = Public Switched Telephone Network

Table 1–3. Network speed and transfer times for a 10 MB file using different networking technologies

networks that are capable of handling interactive media traffic in both local and wide-area environments.

For the near term, companies will continue to use CD-ROMs to send large interactive media files to field personnel. All of the networking options are acceptable for sending the relatively small files associated with pricing and competitive information and other text files. Most companies will continue to use both CD-ROMs and modem or ISDN technologies to send information to the field until ATM services are available on a widespread basis at a reasonable cost. At the current pace of deployment, this is not likely to occur until the turn of the century.

Business Managers and Technology

Ninety-seven percent of the managers surveyed by *Information Week* magazine indicated that understanding information technology (IT) was important to their companies, and 69 percent felt that IT creates business opportunities for their companies. These executives feel that they must be able to understand opportunities that emerge because of changes in technology. By so doing, business people can be more responsive to the changing needs of their businesses.

This shift bodes well for interactive media in business. Technically savvy business managers will understand the difference that interactive media capabilities can make in business processes. They'll understand that performance support systems can improve customer service, increase sales, and improve decision making. When interactive media are put in a business context that is meaningful to these managers, they will make the decision to invest.

Many technology managers are educating themselves about business and hiring people who can work in both the business and technology domains. IT managers recognize that rather than dwelling in the technology they must become intimate with the operation of the business if they are to provide sound advice to business management.

Studies by the Institute for Information Studies[2] noted that IT managers were pursuing the following activities to close the gap by:

- ❏ Adding an educational component to formal information systems functions
- ❏ Ensuring that the chief information officer (CIO) understands the business and is able to relate technology advances to business operations
- ❏ Figuring out how to get value from investments in emerging technologies
- ❏ Deploying technology that satisfies the vision of the chief executive
- ❏ Providing education and demonstrations (e.g., prototyping systems)

Tactical → Strategic

Information technologists are moving from a tactical (cost saving) to a strategic (revenue generating) mode of operation, from standalone applications to business processes. The use of technology is being driven by overall business needs rather than the need to improve efficiency and lower costs.

Vendors and Business

In the early days of the information technology era, vendors knew how, where, and why their technologies satisfied their customers' business needs. They were able to teach their customers how the technology worked because they had already learned how to take advantage of technology in specific applications. In the computer and telecommunications markets, product improvements meant cost reductions. New and improved technologies were applied in individual departments to save time and money.

Unfortunately, many vendors did not change their approach; they are still selling technology when they should be partnering with their customers to help them use new technologies to realize fundamental business goals. The issue is not how fast the processor operates or how much memory the latest personal computer provides, but rather how it can be used to effect improvements in business processes.

All too often, personal computers were purchased based on the strength of their technical specifications and not on the ability of a hardware/software suite to satisfy the tasks of the individuals in business processes. In some companies, executives were given the most powerful computers, and information knowledge workers were given the least powerful computers. An examination of the business processes would likely indicate that it should have been the other way around.

For all parties, the situation has been aggravated by the rapid pace of technological change. And it has been complicated by the use of groups and teams that cross organizational boundaries as corporations look for ways to improve core business processes.

Vendors must learn to shift their relationships with both business and technology managers. The technological push doesn't satisfy the needs of the business community unless it can be related to improving the business process. And yet there is an inexorable push by business to ensure that it takes advantage of leading-edge technologies, that it takes advantage of new business opportunities and responds to competitive threats.

Closing the Gaps: In Conclusion

Three actions are needed to close the gaps between the three communities—business groups, information technology groups, and interactive media vendor and developer communities:

1. Vendors must develop partnerships with their clients so they can participate fully in efforts to enhance business processes.

2. Information technologists need to enhance their ability to relate technology to business goals.

3. Senior business managers must be able to relate business goals in terms that both information technologists and vendors can understand.

The key ingredient in the dialogue between the parties is a common understanding of the business process, the goals of the corporation, and the impact that the technology can bring to bear.

REFERENCES

Caldwell, Bruce. 1995. CEOs click on IT. *InformationWeek*. May 8, 1995:29–40.

Champy, James. 1995. *Reengineering management*. New York: HarperBusiness.

Fetterman, Roger L., and Byrne, H. Richard. 1995. *Interactive selling in the '90s*. San Diego: Ellipsys International Publications.

Ghoshal, Sumantra, and Bartlett, Christopher A. 1995. Changing the role of top management: Beyond structure to processes. *Harvard Business Review*. January–February 1995:87–89.

Wang, Charles B. 1994. *Techno vision: The executive's survival guide to understanding and managing information technology*. New York: McGraw-Hill.

NOTES

[1] The term "multimedia or multimedia-capable computers" is in common use in the interactive media industry. I will use the term "interactive media computers" throughout the book. See Chapter 2 for an historical perspective on these terms.

[2] The Institute for Information Studies was established in 1987 by Nortel, in association with The Aspen Institute, to recognize the increasingly significant role and responsibility of executives in leveraging the information assets of their enterprise.

2

Traditional and Emerging Uses of Interactive Media in Business

Before we explore the traditional uses of interactive media in business, it is fitting to review the origins of some of the terms used in this book. All of the terms are computer-centric, beginning with "hyper linkages" and ending with "interactive media." The first manifestation of hyper linkages was "hypertext," which allowed users to move through and between documents simply by clicking on a highlighted word or phrase.

Hypertext is defined in *Webster's College Dictionary* as "a method of storing data through a computer program that allows a user to create and link fields of information at will and to retrieve the data nonsequentially."

Very shortly thereafter, the term "hypermedia," which encompasses all of the six digital media types discussed in the Introduction, came into vogue. Hypermedia is defined in *Webster's* as "a system in which various forms of information, as data, text, graphics, video, and audio, are linked together to form a hypertext program." Hyper linkages are the foundation of the simple and powerful navigation scheme on the Web. Users can move from page to page simply by clicking on highlighted text or graphic elements.

The term "multimedia" became popular because multiple media, including audio and video, could be mediated on personal computers. Although the term "interactive" is not always included, it is important to note that interactivity is present in all of these terms. Computer-based training was originally known as interactive multimedia training. Throughout the rest of the book, I will use the term "interactive media" to include any and all of its predecessors.

Interactive Media in Business

Although interactive media have the potential to revolutionize the way that information and knowledge are communicated in business, their use in business has largely been confined to relatively few, standalone applications: training, business presentations, information or transaction kiosks, and electronic publication and documentation applications.

This is not to say that applications such as computer-based training, interactive media presentations, and hypermedia documents and publications do not have value. However, it is important to recognize that interactive media have just begun to enter the business mainstream market for use in day-to-day operations.

Computer-based training (CBT) satisfies the need to make training cheaper, faster, and/or better, but it does not address the need to improve the overall performance of an organization. Generally, traditional training, no matter how effective, only brings workers to a basic level of competency. Often, it does not adequately prepare them to handle the variety of real-world situations they will actually encounter on the job.

Hypermedia documents can solve problems of information search, retrieval, and presentation and reduce documentation costs, but they do not ensure improved competency. Even by combining CBT and hypermedia documentation, the result only deals with a subset of an employee's job.

Multimedia sales presentations can be incredibly compelling, but unless their use is consistent with the customer's buying and the vendor's selling processes, they may not help close more orders or generate greater revenues.

The good news is that large companies such as Apple Computer, Boeing Aircraft, Booz•Allen & Hamilton, Federal Express, Herman Miller, Marriott Hotel, Holiday Inn, and Storage Technology Corporation are moving interactive media capabilities into the mainstream of their business operations. Their involvement with interactive media is not confined to training, presentations, or electronic documentation, but is extended to the more complete, more powerful, and more effective solutions offered by performance support systems.

Performance support systems focus on improving the competency of an organization on an overall results-oriented basis rather than on improving achievement in a single task area. The realization of the opportunity must begin and end with the following if we are to ensure that the desired results are achieved:

❑ An examination of business processes

❑ Establishment of measurable results

❑ Determination of how to apply technology

For example, if compelling product presentations are critical to closing an order, then the capability of producing high-quality, interactive media presentations should definitely be included in the sales performance support system. If the resulting presentations have no significant impact on the sales process, they should be disregarded. An accurate analysis of the stages and the individual activities in each stage of a particular business process will reveal the activities that are critical to the success of the process and how interactive media may help in achieving that success.

The successful bid by Atlanta, Georgia, for the 1996 Olympic Games was due in no small part to the use of interactive media presentations. Atlanta provided all of the important facts and personally addressed the concerns of the members of the selection committee. Members of the committee were able to interact with the presentation to satisfy their need to know that Atlanta was providing the best proposal.

In many businesses, a current dilemma that directly affects Apple Computer and the Macintosh platform is the failure to distinguish between vertical or *cost-driven* and horizontal or *revenue-driven* strategies in corporations. An article in the October 30, 1995 issue of *MacWEEK* noted that several companies were embracing the Macintosh more fully while others had decided to move to an Intel-based platform.

The major reason for the shift to Intel/Microsoft was cost savings, since the companies would need to support only a single desktop platform. The fact that independent studies (such as the one conducted by the Gartner Group, illustrated in Figure 2–1) have determined that the cost of ownership of the Macintosh is *less* than the Intel/Microsoft platform did not carry the day.

Suppose that the Macintosh is the best platform for a given core business process—one that contributes to the bottom line by increasing profitability and velocity to market. In this case, the decision should be based on the merits of the hardware/software combination for achieving the goals of the process. The contribution of the investment to improving the business process is the key. In this case, the overall cost of supporting personal computers in the corporation is not the critical factor.

Business processes are also living, breathing entities carried out by human beings. Successfully applying interactive media to business processes means not only making good choices initially, but continually gathering and responding to feedback from those who use the technologies.

The sections that follow briefly introduce some current business applications. More detailed information and analysis is included in Chapter 3 in the section that discusses market structure by business process.

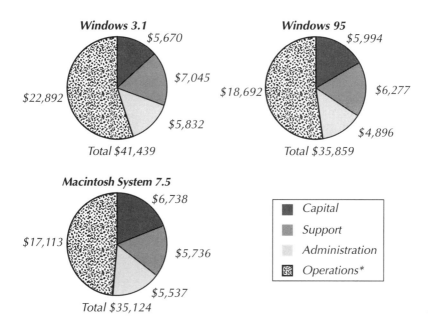

*Soft cost associated with the time users spend to keep desktop computers up and running

Figure 2–1. Five-year cost of ownership of personal computers
Source: Gartner Group

Traditional Interactive Media Business Applications

Computer-based training and business presentations have been the mainstay of interactive media applications for some time now. The persuasive power of audio and video was recognized as significant in both application environments in the early days of interactive media. The interactive use of photo-realistic images and/or dynamic, real-world media such as audio and video moved the information consumer closer to "experiencing the information." This cannot easily be achieved using static media such as text or graphics.

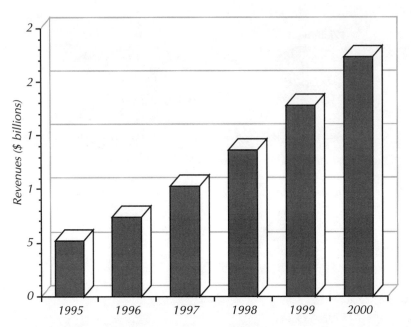

Figure 2–2. Total spent on business applications of interactive media   *Source: Market Vision, 1996*

The value of CBT and interactive media presentations has been demonstrated in numerous applications and is the reason they rank as the top standalone applications. The total spent on traditional interactive media applications is shown in Figure 2–2.

Electronic documentation and publishing have enjoyed dramatic growth because of two phenomena: (1) CD-ROM technology and (2) access to the Internet and more recently the World Wide Web to anyone with a personal computer and a modem.

Computer-Based Training

According to an annual survey by *Training* magazine, corporations in the United States budgeted $52.2 billion for formal employee training in 1995. The survey results indicated that

49.6 million employees will receive some kind of employer-provided training in 1996.

Computer-based training encompasses interactive training, customer support and training, distance learning, and performance support systems. It involves the use of interactive media capabilities to educate, train, and inform individual employees so that productivity and performance are enhanced.

As shown in Figure 2–3, total expenditures on interactive media business training, including performance support systems, will grow from $1.9 billion in 1995 to $4.3 billion in the year 2000. This market represents a substantial business opportunity for companies involved in corporate training.

Many organizations are facing a dilemma. There are more people to train, the amount of course material is increasing, and there are fewer dollars per student available for training. With traditional classroom training, there is no way to leverage

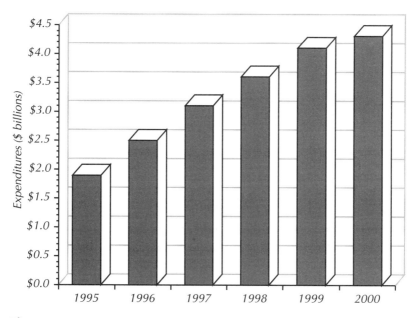

Figure 2–3. U.S. expenditures on interactive media business training   *Source: Market Vision, 1995*

training resources—overall training hours, time, and money rise in direct proportion to the number of people who need to be trained.

Self-paced interactive CBT has been used by many organizations with increasing frequency over the past 20 years because it generates measurable results. Research by Brandon Hall of the *Multimedia Training Newsletter* indicates that:

- ❏ CBT can reduce the total cost of training when compared to instructor-led training.
- ❏ CBT generally requires less time for training compared to instructor-led training.
- ❏ CBT can result in equal or higher-quality learning over traditional instruction.

More specifically, a number of organizations[1] studied the benefits that can be realized using interactive training solutions rather than classroom training over a six-year period. They concluded that:

- ❏ Understanding and retention increased.
- ❏ Training time was compressed by 38 to 70 percent.
- ❏ Students were able to master the content 60 percent faster.
- ❏ Content retention was 25 to 50 percent higher after up to 30 days.

Industry experts note that the value of training increases as it moves *closer* to the workplace of the trainees. Training shifts to *learning* when it is made available where and when people are doing their jobs. Just-in-time learning or performance support systems recognize that each employee is extraordinary, with unique work experience and individual ways of learning. Employees are constantly experiencing changes in work requirements and information needs.

Performance support systems provide people with whatever supports they need to perform their jobs competently

(Malcolm, 1992). Typically, performance support systems provide access to information (including how to structure and accomplish various tasks), advice, and training. In this case, training is usually in the form of small modules that are focused on applications—case studies or practice exercises. The individual can access training material when he or she needs to handle a particular on-the-job situation.

Increased emphasis is being placed on the use of performance support systems to provide access to corporate knowledge bases. A knowledge base is a database that is the collective know-how of the corporation. It is the "best thinking" in a consulting firm such as Booz•Allen & Hamilton. It is the engineering rules that determine how and where 540 options can be added to McDonnell Douglas helicopters to suit the needs of its customers. It is the engine configuration information that Deere Power Systems Group uses to design custom engine solutions right at customer locations. A knowledge base is a repository for the intellectual assets of the corporation that must grow and change as individual employees learn.

As noted above, corporations spend large amounts of money on training and learning systems, and it is likely that training budgets will continue to grow throughout the decade and into the 21st century. The training industry and its clients are looking for ways to reduce the cost of training and increase its effectiveness. Each attempt to improve the learning process does not mean that the old method must be eliminated. Even though computer-based training offers some distinct advantages, instructor-led training continues to be used for some courses. The use of CBT will also continue even though performance support systems will be used more widely in the future. As shown in Figure 2–4, various forms of training and learning systems coexist now and will likely continue to coexist in the future.

Each new effort offers some advantage over existing systems, but none has been universally adopted as the final solution. As a result, corporations may use all of the types of training and simply select one based on its merits for the particular situation.

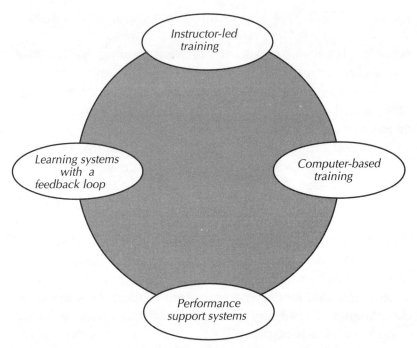

Figure 2–4. The multiple types of training and learning systems in corporations

Multimedia Business Presentations

Presentations are used by almost all information knowledge workers in the corporation to inform, teach, motivate, get approval to proceed, and sell products and services. Regardless of the objective, success is measured by the ability of the presenter to direct the behavior of others toward a desirable course of action or point of view. Multimedia-based presentations can generate a higher level of excitement in the audience and are a more effective way to communicate the right message than traditional text- and graphics-based presentations.

When NASA asked Design Edge to design the interior architecture for the Mars habitat, where six crew members will live for almost a year and a half, one of the deliverables was an interactive media presentation. NASA needed to show Congress and other agencies how the crew members eat, work, exit, and enter the Mars habitat.

The MarsBook application lets the presenter or viewer examine the interior and exterior of the station in several ways. Viewers can see floor plans or renderings, and they can click on objects to rotate them or see how they work—for example, how doors open and panels flip down. All objects in the application are three-dimensional.

Viewers can also take interactive "walk-throughs" of the Mars station by viewing QuickTime movies. Viewers control the direction of movement and the speed of the walk-through, and simply click on an object to interrupt the tour so they can see a full-screen, 24-bit color image of the specific area.

The MarsBook application even lets viewers determine if they've missed anything. Objects that have been clicked for examination are identified by a blue dot on the back of the object. An empty circle on an object indicates that the object has not been examined.

Electronic presentations can be customized for individual audiences with much more effective results. Armed with notebook computers and an interactive media database, sales representatives can tailor their presentations to include customer-specific elements. This capability can eliminate the stigma of the "canned" presentation that tries to be all things to all people.

Business presentations are not confined to the conference room. Information about employee benefits programs can also be delivered using kiosks at various locations. Product presentations are delivered at retail stores to allow the client to browse through a catalog. Home pages on the World Wide Web (Web) often include product presentations that can be viewed in real time or downloaded for viewing later.

In networked interactive media environments, individuals at various locations in a company can log on to the same presentation. Usually, networked presentations are set up and controlled by a moderator, but control can be passed to each viewer. All parties can communicate by sending messages to all of the other participants.

As shown in Figure 2–5, the amount spent on interactive media business presentations in 1995 was $1.4 billion. Both

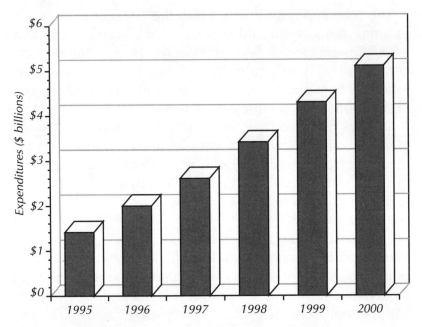

Figure 2–5. U.S. expenditures on interactive media business presentations
Source: Market Vision, 1995

training and business presentations are valuable but have tended to be standalone applications. We will explore the importance of the shift that occurs when training becomes part of a performance support system and presentations become part of the sales process.

Kiosks

The research firm Dataquest, Inc., of San Jose, California, estimates that revenues generated by kiosk vendors will reach $2 billion by 1999, based on 250,000 units shipped as shown in Figure 2–6.

Kiosks are being used by government and business organizations as a new way to provide information and services. In government, kiosks provide a convenient way for job applicants to find and review job openings or for constituents to find out about unemployment benefits, worker retraining programs, and other services. In some states,

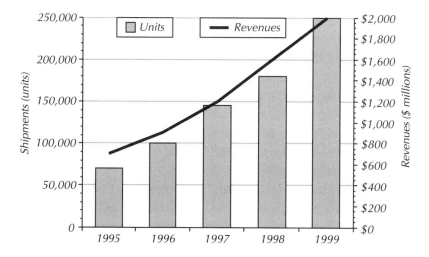

Figure 2–6. Forecasted interactive media kiosk unit shipments and revenues

Source: Dataquest, San Jose, CA

kiosks provide legal information and automate certain legal processes, such as no-fault divorces, vehicle registration, driver license renewal, and payment of parking tickets.

In business, kiosks are being deployed as point of sale (POS) devices for automobiles, baseball tickets, compact discs, office products, and a host of other products and services. They are also being used as point-of-information (POI) devices in public places or at trade shows, where they provide information on local goods and services.

Kiosks are being deployed in corporations to deliver information to relatively large numbers of potential users. Many companies are beginning to use kiosks to provide employee access to employment opportunities, benefits packages, and retirement programs. These systems are usually justified because they reduce the need for clerical and administrative personnel.

Kiosks are also being applied to help companies conduct business with their customers. Alamo Rent A Car has been using kiosks to process reservations. Alamo finds the customer's reservation, authorizes the charge, allocates and locates the car, and prints out the rental contract. Customers need not wait in line at a rental counter.

Chrysler is test-driving Modus, a touch-screen kiosk, at MidPark Jeep-Eagle, Inc., a dealership in Dallas, Texas. Potential buyers can find information about new cars and the fixed price tags they carry. Consumers who want to comparison shop can access automotive sites on the Web from the Modus kiosks. In addition, the kiosks will print a bar-coded label on a sheet that contains directions and a map to MidPark. At MidPark, customers can insert the bar-coded printouts into one of the kiosks at the dealership to obtain the exact lot location of the car they want to see. On average, the time to sell a car is being reduced from 4 hours and 55 minutes to less than an hour. Previously, a salesperson, a sales manager, and a finance and insurance staffer were involved in the sales process. With the Modus kiosk, one person is able to handle the entire transaction (King, 1996).

Bandag, Inc., in Muscatine, Iowa, produces and sells pre-cured tread rubber and equipment used by its franchisees for retreading tires. Bandag wanted to convey its new corporate strategy to 1,300 international franchisees during a 10-day sales conference on the island of Maui. Bandag business owners were able to review their company's future plans throughout the conference at kiosks designed by Ikonic Interactive, Inc., of San Francisco, California.

In addition, attendees used the touch-screen interface to review new products, warranty information, and new regulations; make amortization calculations; and watch the new products in action. The kiosks proved to be an intriguing vehicle for introducing franchised dealers, who are all independent small businessmen, to complex, sophisticated products.

Throughout the conference, Ikonic employees captured newsworthy items and responses from attendees using video cameras. This new content was digitized, edited, and loaded into the kiosks before the start of each new day. The easy-to-use interface is shown in Figure 2–7.

Telecom '95, the world's largest telecommunications conference, is held once every four years in Geneva, Switzerland.

Figure 2–7. Screen shot from a kiosk used by franchisees at the Bandag sales conference

Source: Bandag, Inc., Muscatine, Iowa

It provides an opportunity for vendors such as GTE to display a variety of products and services to an international audience.

With more than 22 million access lines in six countries, GTE is the fourth-largest publicly held telecommunications company in the world and the largest U.S.-based local telephone company.

Ikonic Interactive, Inc., a leading San Francisco-based interactive media firm, teamed with GTE VisNet to create an interactive capabilities presentation on a touch-screen kiosk. The companies decided to use MPEG and video-server technology to deliver full-motion, full-frame, high-quality video.

After watching a video, conference participants were given an opportunity to enter information about their communications needs. The kiosks were programmed to monitor the activities of the participants while they were browsing through still images, animations, illustrations, and videos. When visitors touched the "more information" button, the kiosks alerted a GTE representative.

All of the information provided by the participants was relayed to the GTE representatives, who were able to greet and respond in person—in less than five minutes.

Daisytek International Corporation of Plano, Texas, sells name-brand office automation consumables such as printer and copier supplies, inkjet cartridges, printer ribbons, diskettes, and accessories. The company distributes more than 6,000 products to 20,000 customer locations, including value-added resellers, computer supply dealers, computer and office product superstores, and other retailers that resell to end users. Daisytek is trialing an office products kiosk, under the brand name Supplies Express™, on behalf of retailers at several CompUSA and Office Depot stores across the country. The kiosks contain information about more than 5,000 SKUs.

Daisytek recognizes that rapid evolution of technology in the computer and office market presents a growing problem to retailers. In retailing, both shelf and inventory space are expensive and must be managed carefully. The proliferation of new consumables for updated products forces retailers to move old products off the shelf and ultimately out of the warehouse. Thus the users of older products may find it difficult to locate and purchase consumables.

The Supplies Express kiosks are an exemplary solution for all parties. Customers are assured that retailers with Daisytek kiosks will be able to provide supplies for new as well as older products. Retailers are able to satisfy the needs of their customers for new and older products without increasing shelf or storage space and expense. And, finally, Daisytek is able to serve the needs of both its retail channels and their customers.

Customers can search for a product by general category, brand name, or manufacturer part number, or they can use a free-form search. If the product is in stock, the kiosk provides a product locator guide. Orders can be placed for in-stock items as well as for out-of-stock and hard-to-find items.

Customers at CompUSA stores can use credit or charge cards by swiping them in a card reader in the kiosks. The kiosks accept Visa, American Express, MasterCard, and Discover cards. At Office Depot stores, the kiosks print out a sales ticket that customers present to the cashier for payment. In either case, Daisytek receives the orders electronically and ships the products to the customer by FedEx® delivery service.

A built-in microphone allows customers to speak to a product expert when they press a help button. When the kiosk is idle it reverts to an advertising loop. Daisytek

Approximately 75 percent of the CD-ROM title revenues in 1995 were derived from institutional sales, which include professional, corporate, library, educational, and in-house publishing. Corporations are catching on to the value of CD-ROM for archiving material currently stored on microfiche or microfilm or paper. Many companies deliver their product documentation on CD-ROM. The Social Security Agency (SSA) has placed its 30,000-page Procedures and Operations Manual System (or POMS) on a single CD-ROM.

Other organizations such as RDC Interactive Media and Hanley-Wood, Inc., have elected to take advantage of CD-ROM capabilities to convert a valuable paper-based product—each April issue of *Builder* magazine—to an even more valuable electronic document. Like the printed version, the annual *Guide to Building Products* on CD-ROM contains information about products available from 2,100 suppliers in the form of product literature, catalogs, and video clips. Now 30,000 builders, remodelers, and architects can quickly locate the information they're looking for by searching the product categories on the CD-ROM (see Figure 2–9).

Suppose a builder sees an ad in a magazine for a bath/shower combination that is ideal for a home under construction. The paper ad provides a limited amount of information about the unit and probably a toll-free number. The CD-ROM version could provide pictures of the unit with several color schemes, complete installation information, and the names and addresses of local suppliers.

As shown in Figure 2–10, the builder could also browse through the Masco product section to look for high-quality faucets that match the bath/shower combination that was selected previously.

Builders, remodelers, and architects are qualified buyers. They want to buy the kinds of products that are advertised in *Builder* magazine, but paper-based documents do not provide enough information for them to complete the transaction. The CD-ROM version, or a Web-based version, can provide all of the descriptive information, specifications, and color schemes.

The key to this success story stems from the decision to start with something that works and to make it work even

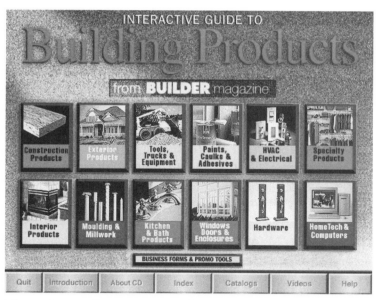

Figure 2–9. The viewer can choose from 12 product categories on the main menu of the interactive guide.
Source: RDC Interactive Media, Palo Alto, CA

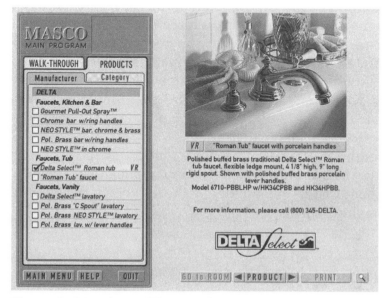

Figure 2–10. The Building Products CD-ROM provides access to complementary products from multiple vendors.
Source: RDC Interactive Media, Palo Alto, CA

better for the target audience. *Builder* magazine serves an audience of 225,000 builders. The 1997 *Guide to Building Products* on CD-ROM will go to 40,000 builders, and a new Web site will reach 25,000 builders. The reach of the CD-ROM and the Web site is limited only by the number of builders with a CD-ROM player and the number with a modem on their personal computers, respectively.

Electronic publishing of information has grown even more rapidly with commercial use of the World Wide Web. More than 40 percent of large public corporations in the U.S. have established Web sites that provide information about the company, recent news and financials, and product and service information. Many expect that their home page will enable them to provide a new information channel to existing and potential customers.

Anyone who has attempted to research the products and services offered by vendors, or their financial performance, will find that it is decidedly easier to find information about target companies by searching the Web than by contacting the company directly. Although it is possible to obtain copies of annual reports and other material, it is not always easy to reach the appropriate parties; surface mail is relatively slow, and once you get the material you need to search it manually. You do not have access to keyword searches and other computer-aided search mechanisms as you do with electronic documents. In the long run, electronic media will become the vehicle of choice for corporations and individuals to exchange information.

In addition, corporations hope that the Web will be an effective means of advertising and promoting their products and services. This is discussed in the section on the Internet later in this chapter.

Emerging Applications

The traditional applications—interactive training and presentations—have consistently validated the real worth of interactive media capabilities: enhancement of the communication of information and the transfer of knowledge. Almost all of the measures established through a number of scientific studies support this conclusion. More recently, electronic documentation and publication have improved the accessibility of information and dramatically reduced costs. Cost reduction tends to be the driving force.

However, it is appropriate to examine the distinctions that arise when interactive media capabilities are applied in core business operations or business processes. In many cases, the media-rich environment that can be offered by interactive media is not a prerequisite for success. Interactive text and graphics may be all that is required. However, interactive media allow us to move from *standalone* to *mainstream* business applications. As a result, interactive media can be linked to improved profitability, improved products, better customer service, faster time to market, and other corporate goals in addition to cost reduction.

Corporate know-how can be made available to individuals in the context of their jobs wherever and whenever they need it. As part of performance solutions, knowledge bases, which contain the intellectual assets of the corporation, are accessible 24 hours per day, 365 days per year. Information knowledge workers need not wait until an expert returns their calls or responds to an e-mail message since they can access the information directly.

In this venue, interactive media capabilities demonstrate greater value because their application can be linked directly to business goals and measurable results. The case studies below, as well as those in Chapters 3 through 7, will contrast the benefits of performance support systems and standalone applications. The following systems exemplify efforts to apply interactive media capabilities to business processes.

Sales Performance Solutions

Interactive selling systems improve the productivity of sales representatives by providing just-in-time access to integrated information, know-how, and learning modules.

Typically, these systems comprise some or all of the following elements:

- Multimedia product and/service catalogs
- Modules for preparing and delivering presentations
- Configuration and quotation or proposal preparation tools
- Expert systems based on corporate knowledge bases
- Interactive learning modules
- Territory management systems
- Reference materials

Since sales and marketing expenses account for 15 to 35 percent of total corporate costs on average, the successful deployment of sales performance systems and solutions has been a desirable objective for more than a decade. Although they are often called sales automation systems, they do not automate the sales process but instead enhance it. The desired outcome is to enhance the process and thereby improve performance—resulting in increased sales and customer satisfaction.

The sales force in the United States is huge; an estimated 20 percent of the work force is involved in some type of sales and marketing activity. The advent of global competition, along with increasing numbers of products and increased complexity of products, has heightened the interest of corporations in using interactive media to improve sales and contain costs.

The availability of interactive media laptop computers with the functionality, power, memory, and storage capabilities of desktop computers, combined with vastly improved data communications systems, has spurred increasing interest in sales performance solutions. Sales is the first business process that is incorporating interactive media capabilities on a widespread basis.

As an example, the Deere Power Systems Group found that the lack of timely information was a roadblock to business growth. Deere's sales performance solution combined interactive media product presentations with a real-time product configurator which enables sales representatives to provide accurate, custom engine solutions at customer locations. The benefits included more profitable unit sales, a shorter sales cycle, and increased customer satisfaction.

Although the implementation of successful sales performance solutions has been a demanding task, with more failures than successes, the value of interactive media capabilities can be clearly demonstrated through a return on investment (ROI) analysis. In order to do the ROI analysis, it is necessary to thoroughly understand the selling process to determine where interactive media capabilities can be applied in order to achieve measurable goals consistent with corporate objectives.

Apple Computer learned that interactive media presentations and instant access to product information were key ingredients in their efforts to sell Macintosh computers. The Apple Reference, Performance, and Learning Expert (ARPLE) system provides instant access to all the digitized content needed by Apple's distribution channels.

Just throwing interactive media technology at sales representatives does not work, but showing them how interactive media capabilities can improve the selling process is a proven winning scenario. Sales people will take advantage of tools that help them close orders more quickly and more often.

As George Colombo noted in his book *Sales Force Automation*, "the objective of sales force automation is not to substitute technology for the skills of the sales professional, but rather to put tools in that professional's hands which augment and enhance his or her skills" (Colombo, 1994).

Gannett determined that it could regain some of the newspaper advertising revenues lost to other media and direct mail by combining advertising page layout, graphics, and page design with customer order information on a Macintosh PowerBook laptop computer. Sales executives can greet prospective clients with tailored interactive media presentations, sample ads, and rate schedules and then submit their orders directly to corporate computers with the click of a button.

According to the International Data Corporation (IDC), a leading provider of market information and industry analysis, 80 percent of the Fortune 1000 are actively pursuing or planning some form of sales performance solution. Although the opportunity is large, it is important to note that a significant number of sales performance projects fail because of poor planning, lack of understanding of the sales process, trying to do too much, and failing to secure the cooperation of the sales force.

Carpet One, an 11-store retail carpet chain in Pennsylvania, was able to cut costs by producing advertisements and marketing materials in-house. Based on its initial success with Macintosh computers, the company decided to develop a sales information system to improve customer service. Newton MessagePads contain all of the information needed by sales representatives to allow them to determine which specific products are available and to calculate prices on the spot.

A sales performance solution succeeds when it is directed at measurable business goals, such as increased sales and gross profit margins, reduced costs, and enhanced competitive positioning. Since buying and selling are (hopefully) complementary processes, it is imperative that both are thoroughly understood before proceeding. The aim of a sales performance solution should be to facilitate the work of the sales force so it can readily and effectively respond to customer needs and improve the sales process—ultimately increasing sales.

Just-in-Time Learning and Reference

Just-in-time learning and reference is another example of a performance support system. Information, knowledge, and tools are made accessible to employees in the context of their daily tasks when and where they are needed. The performance solution is directed at the real-world situations that employees meet on the job.

As noted by Lance Dublin of the Dublin Group in San Francisco, memorization and instructor-led training can now be replaced by much more effective performance support systems. Most of the information and tools needed by employees can now be made available on demand. Computer and communications technologies can be combined with digitized content to provide the information/knowledge delivery equivalent of the just-in-time factory production model.

Dublin notes that traditional, instructor-led training costs average $150 to $350 per student per day. In addition, companies incur lost productivity as employees wait to be trained or spend time away from their jobs. Most companies spend between 1 and 5 percent of their total budgets on employee training. Dublin is an advocate for performance support systems since learning, guidance, and support are embedded in the application itself or are accessible from the application at any time.

The information in Table 2–1 was prepared by the Dublin Group to provide a direct cost comparison between a traditional approach and one using an Integrated Performance Support System (IPSS) to train 500 employees.

In a factory environment, just-in-time learning and reference can be used to train individual workers to execute a new step in the process, to build a "customer-specific" unit, or to integrate a new component into the final product. Once the employee has completed the learning module, he or she can be certified to handle the new manufacturing process.

Performance support systems can also be used in banking. Banc One Corporation of Columbus, Ohio, has established the best record for returns on assets and equity in banking, despite a long period of expansion (the addition of more than 100 banks since 1968) that has made it one of the largest bank holding companies in the United States. The company expanded through carefully targeted acquisitions and savvy deployment of computer and communications technology and digitized content.

Branch automation and teller support systems are implemented at 1,350 Banc One branch offices. The performance support system contains reference, simulation, instruction, and test modules. Learning materials, which are part of the

	Traditional Approach	IPSS Approach
Lost opportunity cost in the first year	Cost: $2.5 million	Cost: $0 System
Cost incurred while staff waits to be trained	Traditional training occurred over 12 months. Full payback could have been achieved in 6 months, but users had to wait to be trained. Assumes 50% of the six-month payback is lost in the first year.	System was implemented in six months. Training takes place on the job. No time is lost waiting for training.
Lost work time	Cost: $1 million	Cost: $200,000
Time spent training means time is lost from regular duties.	Average cost to employ one person is $1,000 per week (salary + equipment + benefits). If each of the 500 employees gets two weeks of training, it costs the company.	With IPSS, training lasts only two days for each employee
Training expense	Cost: $475,000	Cost: $60,000
What it costs for in-house training	Employing two trainers and setting up a facility to train 500 students in one year costs $375,000. Cost of developing two weeks' worth	Cost for facilitator/coach to help with initial system use
User support (help desk)	Cost: $200,000	Cost: $100,000
The cost to support end users after training	Need two full-time employees (system experts), facility, and equipment	
System development	Cost: $0	Cost: $1 million
Total	$4.17 million	$1.36 million

Table 2–1. Training cost comparison between a traditional approach and an integrated performance support system (IPSS)
Source: The Dublin Group, San Francisco, CA

overall training curriculum, are stored on file servers in each branch so employees can take training modules when they want and need to take them.

The investment in the performance support system results in savings associated with the development and delivery of training and with support costs. Branches no longer need to send employees to outside courses, and the learning cycle has been shortened. The program has allowed Banc One to sustain rapid growth because the training and support system is available to new branches the minute the doors are opened.

The Internet

No book on interactive media capabilities is complete without a discussion about the phenomenon called the Internet. The Internet is "happening" for many of us at a time when interactive media personal computers, 28.8 kbps modems and ISDN access, and browsers with graphical user interfaces are available.

Internet growth has been a source of debate. Although there were estimates as high as 40 million users, most researchers indicate the number is significantly less. At the end of 1995, there were approximately 10 million users and more than six million host computers on 60,000 registered "internetworks." By the end of 1996, the number of adult users had grown to more than 20 million. The growth rate appears to be increasing, with new networks being added every few minutes. Many sources indicate that intranets or private/secured Internet sites will be the fastest growth area because intranets provide a cost-effective mechanism for linking employees in large and small companies.

The Internet offers ubiquitous electronic mail capability which accounts for approximately 20 percent of the traffic. File transfers account for 40 percent, and an additional 30 percent of the traffic is generated by global information searches. Computer users are the recipients of the value of the Internet and commercial on-line services.

The World Wide Web (Web) comprises home pages established by individuals, businesses, and government organizations. Home pages are used to disseminate information, market products, and provide support services to visitors. Home pages must be visually attractive and contain content of value or they fail to attract attention. Enhanced networks are encouraging the operators of Web pages to add interactive media content to their databases.

Corporations are fascinated with the potential that the Internet and the Web offer for advertising and promoting their products, even though they are uncertain about the business models, value chains, and new technologies that are needed to make it a secure place of business. For many companies, the Internet represents latent business opportunities that are real enough to warrant an investment in a home page.

According to a 1995 Forrester Research survey of top executives in Fortune 1000 companies, nearly half the surveyed respondents said their companies will use the Internet for business transactions by 1996, and nearly 70 percent by 1998. Fortune 1000 companies are establishing home pages that provide detailed information about their companies, products, and services and the industries they represent.

Many businesses do not have access to the resources needed to create and maintain a quality presence on the Web. As a result, there is a burgeoning opportunity for individuals who understand how to design Web pages. Poorly designed home pages vanish almost as quickly as they appear. Web users are unforgiving critics of home page design and value.

From a marketing perspective, the Internet is a new medium that is different from magazines, newspapers, radio, and television. The Internet and commercial on-line services require a new set of marketing rules. As noted by Forrester Research, Internet users want access to factual product information. The advertising messages that work well on other media do not work on the Internet. In fact, on-line users have a negative reaction to hype and hyperbole.

The critical difference between on-line marketing and traditional marketing is interactivity. Buyers and sellers can interact. The marketing message is no longer one-way. According to Daniel Janal, owner of Janal Communications, a public relations firm based in Danville, California, a comparison of on-line, mass and direct marketing provides a good perspective of on-line marketing:

❏ *Mass marketing*—Needs a mass market to survive. It reaches consumers through radio, television, newspapers, and magazines. It does best when it sells food, health and beauty aids, beer, and cars.

❏ *Direct marketing*—Needs a highly targeted audience. Consumers are reached through mailing lists. It is a good vehicle for selling credit cards, software, travel services, and catalog goods.

❏ *On-line marketing*—Targets individuals through the Internet or commercial on-line services. The consumer must find the seller. It sells travel, stocks, upscale consumer goods, and computer equipment and software. (Janal, 1995)

Many organizations are not clear about the value of their Web pages. First, the value of a Web page in the context of a business process may not have been established, and second, it is still difficult to measure the impact of the number of "hits" or accesses by individuals browsing the Web. Will hits translate into increased sales or heightened brand awareness?

Some companies brag about the number of individuals who access their home page. What value did the visitor receive? Did the company sell more products or services because of the visit? What will it take to make a home page that delivers measurable value in a particular business process? Companies that advertise and promote products or services or provide information to customers and prospective customers must develop an understanding of what works and what doesn't work and a way of measuring results in this new channel.

A mechanism is needed that unobtrusively gathers information based on user experience and makes it easy for the visitor to provide feedback so the Web page can be improved to match the needs of existing and potential customers. The feedback can be used to improve not only the organization's home page but its products and services as well. Never before has there been such a magnificent opportunity to dialogue with potential buyers on a large scale.

Although large numbers of businesses have established Web sites, relatively few are successfully selling products. In part this has been due to the lack of secure electronic commerce technology. It may also be a reflection of the lack of experience in selling products on the Web. However, the opportunity is worthy of exploration. Companies need to find the best mix of Web technologies and new sales approaches that work for their products and services. Early indications are that customer service will be a key factor in making sales. When companies begin to sell on-line, there will be a concrete measure of the value of their Web site. At present, it is difficult to tell if hits result in sales.

The Federal Express customer Web site is one of the earliest and most celebrated successes of the Internet. The company installed a server in November 1994 that allowed customers to determine the status of their packages without the help of Federal Express employees. Each day thousands of customers access its Web site to determine the whereabouts of their parcels. According to some estimates, FedEx is saving up to $2 million a year in customer service.

Some companies use the Internet as an information warehouse and an alternative to private communications networks—to provide employees free access to the vast array of databases and e-mail services. (Refer to the next section on intranets.)

The databases that are maintained by governments, universities, and corporations provide unprecedented access to information about almost any subject to individuals with the knowledge and skills to find and access them. Never before have large and small businesses had access to such vast storehouses of information—and it's free, at least for the moment.

The linkage to interactive media must be based on the role and value of the Internet in specific business processes.

In an electronic commerce environment, a home page can be a repository of up-to-date information for customers and prospects, a mechanism for the exchange of information between visitors and the company, and an interactive media product catalog for use by customers.

The value of the Internet in this environment can be established by examining the selling process to determine how well the Web site satisfies the customers' needs. For some organizations it may have great value; for others it may not fit at all. As with all interactive media capabilities, the role of the Internet must be evaluated against the requirements of the specific process.

Intranet Applications

Although the Internet and World Wide Web have captured the attention of companies around the world, the number of users as a percentage of the total population is still quite small. However, there is another phenomenon based on the use of Internet technologies in companies that is called the *intranet*. Intranets provide an opportunity to enhance productivity by sharing information and corporate know-how and supporting collaboration.

Individuals and groups can access the collective know-how of the company to achieve world-class performance. The information and knowledge of company experts can be made available to anyone who needs it 24 hours per day, 365 days per year. And it can be made available to trusted partners and suppliers outside the company on a worldwide basis.

In a sales environment, an intranet home page can be a repository of up-to-date information for sales representatives and a mechanism for the exchange of information between members of the sales force. However, interactive media product catalogs are usually distributed to remote sales offices on CD-ROMs.

Many corporations already have the networking infrastructure needed to support their own intranets for interactive media applications. Once they install servers and software they can be up and running. Intranets are very desirable because they change the information stored in the mysterious domain of corporate databases into formats anyone can use.

A number of forecasters note that intranets are growing faster than the Internet. This is attributed to the fact that the business rationale for intranets can be directly linked to corporate goals and objectives. Intranets can enhance the communication of information and the transfer of knowledge throughout a corporation. They enable individuals and teams to work together. They enable companies to collaborate with partners and suppliers.

Like the Internet, intranets provide access to the information stored in enterprise databases, on file servers, and on desktop computers. The challenge is to be able to find specific information in an environment where the volume of information can be huge. Search engines that were developed for the Internet are being adapted for intranet applications.

For example, Digital Equipment is providing modified versions of its AltaVista Internet search engine for corporate intranets. If information is the corporate gold, the search engine is the mining equipment that lets us find and extract the gold quickly and easily. It is an enabling technology for both the Internet and intranets.

Intranets dramatically reduce the need for and the cost of paper-based communications. But the big payoff will come from enhancing the business processes that take advantage of the key attributes of an intranet—the ability to find and share information and collaborate with business colleagues.

Some companies plan to use intranets for desktop video-conferencing and collaborative computing. For example, Bear Stearns & Co. intends to use its intranet for videoconferencing so that busy traders and analysts can collaborate without leaving their offices.

Apple's ARPLE and Service Source (see case studies described in Chapters 3 and 5, respectively) are good examples of the value of intranets since they provide access to information and corporate know-how. In both cases, sales and service personnel have access to up-to-date information and know-how regardless of their location. The case studies clearly indicate that access to this information and know-how improves productivity and allows the company to provide better customer service.

There is a caveat at the moment. Companies such as Bear Stearns will use their own network infrastructure to provide the bandwidth needed to support the high bandwidth requirements of videoconferencing. However, many intranets are based on networking infrastructures that cannot support high bandwidth applications.

Field employees who use 14.4 or 28.8 kbps modems or basic rate ISDN to access their intranets will find it too time consuming to download files that are larger than 1 MB. As a result, CD-ROMs will continue to be used to transfer bulk information to employees in the field. Intranets will be used to access volatile information and to collaborate with other employees.

By the end of this century, we will begin to see dramatic improvements in the cost and performance of the public switched network. The new infrastructure will essentially eliminate current bandwidth limitations. However, it will take more than a decade for public network carriers to widely deploy these new networks.

Nonetheless, the Internet and the intranet are powerful agents for change that are available to businesses now.

Pushing the Envelope

Since it is not easy to determine what specific knowledge and/or skills will be relevant to meet the rapidly changing needs of business in the future, the art and science of learning must acquire new levels of adaptability, flexibility, effectiveness, and efficiency. Traditional classroom training and CBT cannot easily be modified to match the accelerating pace of business change in today's global marketplace. This suggests that the business environment of the 21st century will be based on infrastructures that facilitate learning. Success will depend on the ability of organizations to operate effectively even though they are in a state of continuous transformation.

New Levels of Adaptability

*The only sustainable competitive advantage of any organization
(or person) is its ongoing capacity to learn.*
                                              —W. Edwards Deming

Deming's statement presupposes that transformation is no longer a temporary state and that companies will constantly be in transformation. Organizations that learn "how to learn" on a continuous basis will be viable and competitive; those that don't will falter or fall by the wayside.

Overall company performance will depend on how well its employees learn and adapt to their changing environment. Thus the onus is on company management to ensure that the learning needs of its employees are being defined and met at every point in business processes.

Since a company's performance depends to a significant extent on how well it provides for the learning needs of its employees, then it must identify and respond to these needs on an ongoing basis by developing a learning system that automatically adapts itself to the requisite needs of the individual. The latter would be an ideal system for improving learning capacity on the job. The ideal system may not be available now, but companies can take steps in the right direction to meet their changing needs.

The first step is to deploy organizational performance/ learning systems that incorporate a feedback loop to capture new knowledge generated through the use of the system. Learning becomes part of the normal working day, as a tool and source that is shared to increase corporate learning and augment the corporate knowledge base.

The second step is added by learning systems that shift control of the learning experience from the author/designer to the learner. These systems accommodate the "intelligence bandwidth" of the individual rather than providing a "one-size-fits-all" solution. Both are described in the "Enabling the Learning Organization" section that follows.

Performance support systems—designed to assist workers as they work at their jobs—are a step in the right direction.

Learning modules and reference materials can be presented to employees in the context of their jobs when they are needed.

However, performance support systems do not include all of the infrastructure that is needed to facilitate learning. For example, the learning and reference modules of performance support systems are based on a predefined set of needs. There is no built-in mechanism for accommodating the changing needs of the organization. Companies need performance support systems that are capable of responding to changes in learning needs. Performance support systems need to incorporate closed-loop systems that enable them to respond to change.

Corporations can increase the value of organizational systems by evolving them to better match the needs of their constituents. Each step toward completing the closed-loop feedback system increases the capacity of the individuals (and hence, the organization) to learn and generate the sustainable advantage mentioned by Deming. The addition of a formal knowledge-capture process allows the organization to capture the additional knowledge gained by individuals and teams in the performance of their work.

Enabling the Learning Organization

Because many corporations are shifting to multidisciplinary teams, the organizational performance/learning system shown in Figure 2–11 is needed now. The success of these shifts is dependent, to some degree, on the ability of the team to learn from its members.

If the capacity of an organization to learn dictates its long-term viability in the business world, then we need a conceptual framework for how people learn and perform in an organization and mechanisms for capturing and disseminating organizational learning. The approach shown in Figure 2–11, which Barry Raybould refers to as the "Organizational Performance/Learning Cycle," provides such a model (Raybould, 1995).

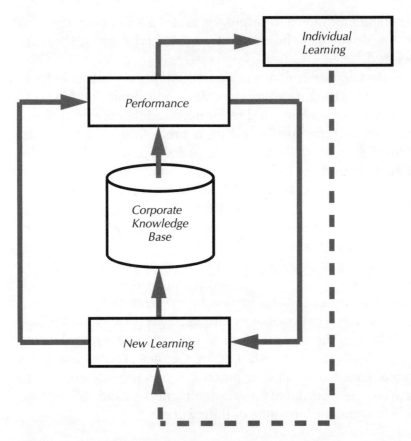

Figure 2–11. The organizational performance/learning cycle
Source: Ariel PSS Corporation, Mountain View, CA

There are five phases to be completed before organizational learning is realized.

1. The company structures a knowledge base and creates an interface to present the knowledge to the employee.

2. The employee achieves the desired performance level by using the system.

3. As a result of ongoing use of the system, the employee internalizes knowledge of the system's behavior. This may occur because the system provides feedback to

the employee in response to incorrect actions. In other cases, learning on the job may immediately precede performance. For example, an employee reviews just-in-time learning modules prior to performing the task.

4. In the course of doing the work, the employee develops new techniques, methods, and procedures that are not part of the knowledge base. However, this new knowledge is only available to the employee at this point.

5. Additional knowledge gained by the employee is captured through a formal process and incorporated into the knowledge base.

Continuation of the cycle back to phase one makes the new knowledge available to the entire organization. Completion of the loop ensures that organizational learning takes place.

To illustrate how the organizational performance/learning cycle might work, let's examine a performance support system for Apple Computer's field service technicians. The system comprises knowledge bases covering the diagnosis and repair of Apple's Macintosh computers and peripheral products. The knowledge bases contain all of the information and know-how available from system designers and senior maintenance personnel. The system contains the best diagnostic and repair practices that are currently available in the company.

A new field service representative uses the knowledge base to diagnose and repair a Power Macintosh 8500/120 computer. Over the course of several weeks, he becomes proficient in the use of the procedures and discovers a short-cut that reduces the time it takes to diagnose and repair a particular fault. Further, he observes that his new procedure ensures that other problems do not mask the fault. This information will be valuable to all other field service personnel. Fortunately, Apple's performance support system includes a process that makes it easy for the technician to capture his improved procedure and include it as an addition to the appropriate knowledge base.

The performance solution just described centers on the design and delivery of a set of software that can carry out each of the five phases described earlier. This wider perspective broadens the definition of a performance solution: A performance solution becomes an electronic infrastructure that captures, stores, and distributes individual and corporate knowledge throughout the organization. It enables individuals to achieve the required level of performance in the fastest possible time with minimal support and intervention from others in the organization.

Based on this new definition, a performance solution:

❏ Encompasses all of the software needed to support the work of individuals

❏ Integrates knowledge assets into the interface of the software tools, rather than including them as add-on components

❏ Satisfies the complete cycle, including the capture and distribution of learning

❏ Includes the management of electronic and non-electronic assets

The new definition allows corporations an opportunity to recognize the strategic importance of managing their knowledge assets. Performance solutions based on the new definition incorporate information technology as an enabler of *learning organizations*.

In many organizations, information technology groups are available to manage and maintain traditional computer databases. However, few corporations have equivalent groups for managing and maintaining the knowledge assets of the company. Without such groups in place, the cycle time for adding additional knowledge may be too slow for the performance solution to be effective.

However, performance solutions are not the final goal conceived by leading learning scientists such as David Boulton of DiaCom Technologies, Inc., of Seattle, Washington. DiaCom's system is a learner-centric system that is user controlled as shown in Table 2–2. In essence, each learner has an

Learning System	Control	Focus	Moment of Need
CBT	Author/designer	Task or function	Not real-time
Simulation	Author/designer	Task or function	Not real-time
EPSS	Author/designer	Task or function	Real-time
DiaCom	Learner	Learning	Real-time

Table 2–2. Comparison between DiaCom's learning approach and traditional computer-mediated systems

interface that enables him or her to achieve mastery over learning goals. The emphasis is placed on each learner's capacity for ongoing learning.

The learning experience with CBT, simulation, and Electronic Performance Support Systems (EPSS) is controlled by the author/designer and it is task- or function-centric. The author/designer determines what will be learned and how it is presented to the student. With CBT and simulation, the learning experiences do not occur at the "moment of need" since students must stop whatever they are doing to take the course they need. EPSS learning modules are available in real time since they are embedded in the performance system that is used on "on the job."

DiaCom Technologies is developing a system that facilitates the process of gathering information about the needs and wants of its stakeholders—customers, employees, and vendors. The system can be embedded in performance solutions, networks, authoring tools, e-mail systems, CBT courses, and any other interactive computer application. The information gathered and processed by DiaCom's Distributed Dialogue Processing™ system can be used by corporations to improve the effectiveness of their systems.

Mr. Boulton has created a general-purpose, electronic, learning-oriented environment that allows learners to explore any body of knowledge in a variety of ways according to their "learning needs." The computer system responds to the learner's curiosity, learning style, and achievement level.

Thus a learner who is exploring computer-based training might encounter performance support systems, become interested in delivery of interactive media content over networks, and end up exploring broadband networking technologies such as ATM and Gigabit Ethernet.

We are witnessing an evolutionary path that is, to some degree, moving toward the master/apprentice form of learning. In this case, the "master" is the collective knowledge and experience of the organization and is made available through computer technology that responds to the individual's intention to pursue a particular line of inquiry. Thus the learning experience follows the best path for the particular individual rather than a generic curriculum established for a large class. Computer-based learning systems, such as CBT or EPSS, have focused on augmenting specific tasks and/or functions and not on "mediating the intelligence of the humans involved."

Corporations that espouse the new definition of performance solutions will establish the hardware, software, and human infrastructures needed to support such solutions. The payback occurs in the form of organizational learning that can improve the company's ability to compete in its chosen markets. According to leading business experts such as Tom Peters and others, organizational learning capability is a key ingredient to success.

REFERENCES

Colombo, George. 1994. *Sales force automation*. New York: McGraw-Hill.

Janal, Daniel. 1995. *Online marketing handbook*. New York: Van Nostrand Reinhold.

King, Julia. 1996. High tech drives automaker's pitch. *ComputerWorld*. February 1996.

Malcolm, Stanley E. 1992. Reengineering corporate training. *Training*. August 1992.

Raybould, Barry. 1995. Performance support engineering: An emerging development methodology for enabling organizational learning.

Notes

[1] Federal Express, IBM, United Technologies, U.S. Army, Wicat Systems, and Xerox.

[2] In this context, broadband refers to the fact that hundreds of megabytes can be delivered on a CD-ROM. In telecommunications, broadband means networks that operate at speeds greater than 1.5 Mbps.

3

Interactive Media Roles in Today's and Tomorrow's Business

The role of interactive media in business can be examined from different points of view: by information users, by application types, or by business processes. Each of these perspectives provides a different view of the potential of interactive media capabilities. Each view provides a different set of insights into the application and the impact of applying interactive media capabilities. But however they are viewed, the overall success of interactive media will still be governed by our ability to deploy its capabilities in business processes.

This chapter is based partly on a market structure first published by the author in *Mainstream Multimedia* (Fetterman and Gupta, 1993). It is included here in modified form because it provides a useful way of looking at interactive media solutions as four different application types:

1. Content-centric (publication or documentation)
2. Presentation-centric
3. Office-centric
4. Operations-centric

The fourth application type—operations-centric—leads to a whole new line of thinking based on the notion that interactive media, or, more specifically, networked interactive media, provide the greatest value in the context of business processes. This notion was confirmed by the research I conducted for *Interactive Selling in the '90s* (Fetterman and Byrne, 1995).

Notwithstanding my conviction that the full benefit of networked interactive media is realized when applied in business processes, significant value has been delivered through standalone interactive media applications in the content- and presentation-centric domain. Accordingly, this chapter will conclude with some noteworthy success stories of content- and presentation-centric applications. One of the applications which began as a content-centric application has evolved to a performance solution.

Information Users/Customers

The information age, which has its roots in the 1970s, has spawned an information technology industry. Yet as a result of the ever-increasing amounts of information being generated, information overload has become a significant problem. Information overload is a critical issue because ever-expanding volumes of information are making it increasingly difficult to find relevant information quickly and easily.

Customers of the information technology industry can be broadly categorized into three groups. These groups are not mutually exclusive, but they do establish the roles of the information customer. The customer may play one or more of the following roles at any particular point in time (Fetterman and Gupta, 1993):

❏ Information consumers
❏ Information presenters
❏ Information knowledge workers

Information Consumers

Everyone in business consumes information in one form or another. We read correspondence and memos, magazines and reports; listen to internal and external presentations; participate in training sessions; or attend conferences. As consumers of information we are informed, educated, asked to do something, promised something, and persuaded to buy products and services or to accept an idea. In some cases we interact with the information that is presented to us. For example, when we listen to a presentation and respond with input, support, or approval, we are interacting with information that is presented.

By definition, the information consumer reviews the information as it is presented and, based on the information, follows a particular course of action. An information consumer does not create new information (except to place an order or request more information) or change it. The information consumer represents the largest set of prospective customers for interactive media products and applications. For the computer industry, the information consumer is potentially any individual who has access to a personal computer. It is highly likely that most information consumers in business environments can have access to interactive media personal computers.

Hypermedia can be of great assistance in dealing with large amounts of information. Hypermedia delivers information in a format that provides multiple connected pathways through a body of information, allowing the user to jump easily from one topic to related or supplementary material, which may be text, graphics, audio, images, or video.

There are tens of millions of information consumers, all of whom are potential customers for the interactive media products created by the computer and consumer electronics industries.

Information Presenters

The second group of information customers is much smaller and consists of people who are subject-matter experts. Information presenters exhibit or create interactive presentations. In most cases, the presenter uses audio/visual equipment such as a slide projector, an overhead transparency projector, or a personal computer and an LCD projection panel.

In the case of an interactive media presentation, the presenter uses an interactive media computer. The interactivity and flexibility of the presentation comprise a significant component of the communication process. For computer-based training (CBT) or point-of-information (POI) kiosks, the rate of information flow and the paths through the presentation are controlled by the user. The information content is usually intended to be of specific interest to a target audience and is presented to small groups.

Business presentations can be delivered by the information presenter, or the user can interact directly with the presentation based on events and branches that are programmed by the subject-matter expert.

In many business environments, both creative and production assistance is available from audio/visual departments. In some cases, the presentation is not prepared by the information presenter but by an individual or a group of experts who are more familiar with the information transfer process and the interactive media development tools.

These software tools, commonly referred to as "authoring tools," are used to create, integrate, and orchestrate interactive media applications. The person who uses an interactive media authoring tool is known as the "author." Authoring software is the glue that binds together the multiple media in interactive media applications.

Previously, when tools were difficult to use, the author was someone who had both creative and technical skills. Now companies such as Apple Computer, Macromedia, and MetaTools have made the authoring tools much easier to use, so that almost anyone can use them to create an interactive media presentation.

Information Knowledge Workers

The third group of information customers is the information knowledge worker. Many office workers today normally use computers to complete work assignments and communicate with co-workers. Information knowledge workers create their own information and receive information from others that is used to make decisions and take action. In some cases, they customize material prepared by others for the specific task at hand. For example, a field sales representative may customize a generic product presentation to suit a specific customer's needs.

In this group, the individuals who create and send messages are most often the same individuals receiving messages from others. They gather, create, and present information continuously in the course of their jobs. *Interactive media add value to the main tasks of information knowledge workers, as they are continually consuming, creating, and presenting information.* This group is less concerned about the media-rich environment of interactive media and more concerned about the interactivity of interactive media.

The number of individuals in this group exceeds the number of information presenters, but it is much less than the number of information consumers. There are millions of office workers with personal computers who are potential customers of interactive media products and services.

Much of the information content is created by the information knowledge worker as part of the on-the-job process. Thus this group buys tools that are designed to assist in the communication of information or transfer of knowledge. The tools needed to facilitate the applications for this group must be simple to use and compatible with widely available personal computers and workstations.

Many developers of software products that are being used by information knowledge workers have added interactive media elements to their products. Electronic mail systems are evolving to include audio and full-motion video. Word processors are evolving to include multiple media to enable them to function as interactive media documentation processors. Spreadsheet programs incorporate voice annotation to enhance their ability to communicate information.

Other developers have created hardware and software elements to support desktop videoconferencing and collaborative computing capabilities. The formation of self-managing teams around information knowledge workers will stimulate demand for conferencing and collaborative products as well as the computing and communications infrastructure needed to support them.

Self-managing teams depend on the exchange of information and knowledge between team members and with members of other teams. Team members are not necessarily in the same location and may include participants from outside the company. For example, during the design of the Boeing 777 aircraft, the teams worked with mechanics and customers to ensure that the aircraft was going to be easy to maintain. Conferencing and collaborative capabilities can be a valuable part of the technology repertoire of self-managing teams.

Market Structure for Interactive Media by Application

When we examine interactive media applications, it is useful to group them into logical units so we can better understand them and determine how they apply to the information customers defined in the preceding sections. Further, we can distinguish interactive media applications in a business context based on the groups shown below:

1. Content-centric applications
2. Presentation-centric applications
3. Office-centric applications
4. Operations-centric applications

Application Type	Customer/User	Creator
Content-Centric Reference material Documentation Information services Education Policies and procedures	Information consumer	Subject-matter expert
Presentation-Centric Business presentation Training Merchandising kiosks	Information consumer (uses the product to receive) Information presenter (uses the product to present)	Subject-matter expert
Office-Centric Word processing Desktop publishing Spreadsheet Mail	Information knowledge worker	Information knowledge worker
Operations-centric Electronic Performance Support System (EPSS) Sales automation Just-in-time training	Integration of: Information consumer Information presenter Information knowledge worker	Subject-matter expert Business operations expert

Table 3–1. Four applications classes cover all of the interactive media applications in the business environment.

Table 3–1 shows the range of applications available in all four segments. For each segment, end users and authors are identified. It is important to distinguish between the professional author and the "casual" business author or information knowledge worker since the roles of each are different.

Interactive presentation-centric applications have been available for more than a decade. In fact, interactive media in business are based largely on presentation-centric applications such as CBT and business presentations. More recently, large numbers of content-centric applications have been developed due to the growing acceptance of CD-ROM technology. CD-ROM and its likely successor, Digital Versatile Disc (DVD) technology, will continue to be used since they provide an inexpensive way to transport large amounts of information—650 MB and from 4.5 to 18 GB, respectively.

Most office-centric application tools are interactive media capable. Word processor and spreadsheet tools allow you to annotate the documents with audio and video clips. Presentation tools allow the presenter to incorporate audio and video clips in addition to graphics, animation, and digitized photographs.

Operations-centric applications, or *performance solutions* as they are referred to in this book, represent the major thrust into the business environment of networked interactive media. The first three applications classes are often combined in the business operations environment, since interactive media can be tailored to suit the needs of the work environment of the individual and the business.

Content-Centric Applications

Content-centric applications are primarily publishing or documentation applications. The information consumer cannot make any changes to the content, although in the case of Web pages individuals can interact, make comments, or ask questions. Many organizations publish product documentation, policy and procedures information, reference material, and other content that has a relatively long half-life (i.e., a month or more).

Information is often made available in hypermedia form so the reader can search for items of specific interest or follow threads through the document that lead to new discoveries. Often, the publisher adds images, audio, and video to make the message more compelling. For example, the conversion of a photo documentary book could include comment by the photographer, descriptive material on the subject of the photographs, and other information that can contribute to the user's overall value of the electronic document.

Content-centric applications have been made possible by the CD-ROM, since an inexpensive vehicle was needed for large amounts (hundreds of megabytes) of interactive media content. Currently, CD-ROM—and in the near term, Digital Versatile Disc—will be the best vehicles for distributing large amounts of information on a periodic basis.

Apple Computer and a number of other large computer companies also use their corporate networks to provide employee access to content-centric applications. Many large corporations have set up Web pages as a means of disseminating information about their organizations, products, recent successes, and other areas to existing and potential customers. Still others set up Web pages with access restricted to employees or customers only. In effect, they are displacing the private networks that would have been needed if the Internet were not available.

In the future, the Internet will become the most effective mechanism for content-centric applications for most corporations, with the proviso that the intended audience has access to the Web.

Presentation-Centric Applications

Presentation-centric applications include training, business presentations, and kiosk-based presentations. Training that takes advantage of interactive media capabilities goes under several different names—among others, self-paced training, computer-based training, and interactive media training. There are many examples which demonstrate the cost savings that result when moving from lecture/lab or instructor-led training to interactive media training.

In addition, conventional training techniques cannot accommodate some training requirements. For example, imagine trying to train a field sales force of 1,500 when a new product line is being introduced. While it is possible to bring them all together, the cost of doing so would exceed $500,000 per day in salaries, travel, and living expenses, plus another $6 million per day in opportunity costs (lost sales) for sales representatives who generate an average $1,000,000 in sales per year. In addition, it would swamp the training staff of the organization. A well-prepared interactive media training course would likely result in a better training experience, and it could take place in between sales calls or at night or over a weekend.

Multimedia presentations can be justified on a standalone basis, but again their value is more meaningful when they are part of a selling process, since the value can be related to the end result—getting the order. The same holds true for kiosks.

The StorageTek and Price Waterhouse case studies at the end of this chapter have more information about justifying interactive media training.

Office-Centric Applications

Multimedia capabilities have been added to existing business and productivity tools. Multimedia offer merely an extension to the tools. Almost all of the word processing, spreadsheet, presentation preparation and delivery, database, utilities, and other tools are interactive media capable.

It is difficult to measure or calculate the value of adding interactive media capabilities to shrink-wrap business and productivity tools until they are placed in the context of business processes. The ability of a spreadsheet or word processing tool to incorporate images, animation, and/or audio or video clips has little merit or meaning unless it is related to increased profitability, reduced cost, enhanced productivity, etc.

In addition, a suite of desktop videoconferencing and collaborating computing tools has been made available for desktop computers. Desktop videoconferencing and collaborative computing are relatively new types of tools that can be applied in any environment to allow individuals or groups to communicate, share, and manipulate content in real time.

While the value of interactive media can be demonstrated on a generic basis, the question in business must always be related to the bottom line. If the addition of a video clip to a series of text instructions shortens the comprehension time and improves retention in a factory floor application, we can measure and establish the value of the reduction in production cycle time.

The value of potential time/travel savings can be determined for desktop videoconferencing and collaborative computing capabilities, but it is not sufficient to support widespread adoption. When individuals can share information on computer screens and talk and see each other at the same time, it is possible to equate the benefits of these capabilities in specific business processes.

The message is clear: establishing the value of interactive media or desktop videoconferencing and collaborative computing must be related either to cost savings in standalone applications or to bottom-line improvements in business processes. Otherwise, such capabilities are not adopted by the mainstream market in a significant way.

Business Operations-Centric Applications

Performance solutions for business processes will be covered in Chapters 5 through 7. The application of interactive media in business is often accompanied by the deployment of client/server technology, high-speed networks, implementation of knowledge databases, data mining systems, etc., all of which may be capable of handling interactive media content.

Business operations-centric applications are an outgrowth of learning how to apply interactive media capabilities in standalone applications and the availability of the enabling technologies previously mentioned, as well as the shift in business from vertical organizational structures to horizontal, process-oriented structures. It is much more difficult to establish the value of interactive media in traditional organizational structures because of the lack of focus on core business processes and measurable goals.

The end result is that many businesses now have the right organizational structure, increased need for improving processes, and access to both the enabling technologies and the know-how to deploy them to satisfy the mission of the corporation.

The case studies below are for content- and presentation-centric applications. Operations-centric case studies are covered in Chapters 5 through 7 for the relevant segments of the four core business processes introduced at the beginning of the book.

Content-Centric Case Studies

Two remarkable case studies covering Apple Computer's Service Source and Lam Research Corporation's Interactive Maintenance System are discussed below. Neither represents a simple conversion of a paper-based system to a hypermedia document. Both companies have evolved the original conversions toward performance support systems since they contain information and know-how of great value to technicians at their place of work. Although neither case study incorporates learning modules, both are a logical extension for the future.

These two examples were included here because the justification of the projects was based on moving from paper-based to electronic documents.

Apple Computer's Service Source

The Situation

What began as an effort to reduce the costs associated with the preparation, distribution, and use of an 18-volume maintenance manual set for service technicians has evolved into a remarkable performance tool. The evolution occurred because the company solicited feedback from field technicians and acted on it to include new features and information on an ongoing basis. Apple Computer sends Service Source CDs to the 5,000 service technicians who maintain and repair Macintosh computers and peripherals around the world.

The Service Source CD contains maintenance manuals consisting of all the information, specifications, troubleshooting procedures, diagnostics, illustrated parts lists, and upgrade information needed to maintain all of Apple's computer and peripheral products. Figure 3–1 is a screen shot of the startup screen that highlights the information available to field technicians. By clicking on the appropriate button, technicians can access the information they need to diagnose and repair a system or to add memory to a new computer.

The troubleshooting and diagnostic procedures lead the technician step-by-step through the process. Photographs are used to illustrate individual tasks in the process. Technicians have access to detailed information about how to disassemble and reassemble the AV module on the Power Macintosh 8500, as shown in Figure 3–2.

Animation and video clips are provided to explain how best to accomplish complex procedures or to illustrate how a product works. For example, the paper path can be shown for a color laser printer by playing a QuickTime movie, as shown in Figure 3–3.

In addition, field representatives can order parts and look up service plans and warranty information. In short, everything

Figure 3–1. The Service Source startup screen provides direct links to the information needed by technicians when and where they need it. [Service Source 2.0 1996]
Source: Apple Computer, Cupertino, CA

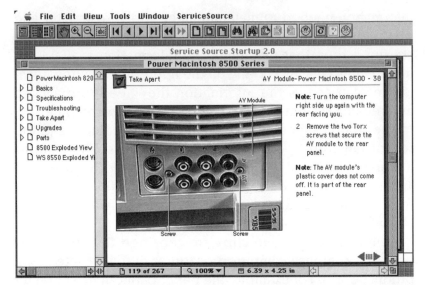

Figure 3–2. Annotated photographs provide the detail needed to repair and maintain all of the components of Macintosh computers. (Service Source 2.0 1996)

Source: Apple Computer, Cupertino, CA

needed to enhance the productivity of field technicians and improve customer service has been transformed from an unwieldy, 18-volume monstrosity to one CD-ROM that is fast and easy to use.

Figure 3–3. The QuickTime movie demonstrates how paper travels through the ColorLaser Writer 12/600PS printer. (Service Source 2.0 1996)

Source: Apple Computer, Cupertino, CA

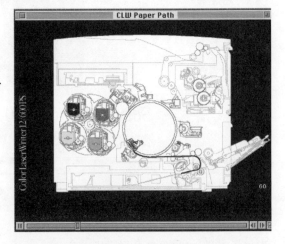

In February 1996, Apple established a Service Source Web site to supplement the information on the CD. The company recognized that it was critical for service businesses to have access to the latest, most up-to-date information. While the Service Source CD will continue to be the main service reference tool, Service Source Online will provide up-to-the-minute information between shipments of update CDs.

Apple's Service Source Web page provides access to the following:

- Hot issues and service notes
- Updates to service manuals
- Reference library
- Service programs
- Software troubleshooting
- Memory upgrades
- Other timely information

Prior to the development of the Service Source CD, a paper-based system was used to inform the independent field technicians who service Macintosh computers and peripheral products. Eighteen technical service procedure manuals contained troubleshooting and repair information and maintenance programs. If the company had not elected to go with Service Source, two more volumes would have been required immediately to cover all of the new products that were being introduced. In addition, more volumes would have been needed as product lines continued to grow in the mid-1990s. The service organization, with support from the finance department, determined that the cost of preparing, printing, handling, storing, and shipping updates to the manuals was excessive.

Previously, updates were prepared and shipped once per month to 5,000 technicians. Each update consisted of 250 pages on average, which meant that the technician was forced to remove 2,500 outdated pages each year and to insert new ones in the affected volumes.

While it was relatively easy to select CD-ROM as the new distribution medium, the selection of the user interface was a task subject to much investigation and trial. Several prototypes with different types of navigational capability were tested. The company chose a highly interactive software tool with a user-friendly interface that provided rapid access to the volumes of technical information on the CD-ROM disk. The new service document is intended for daily use by service technicians and contains more than 200 MB of repair, pricing, and program information that was previously available only in binders and booklets.

Existing text, graphics, and image information were converted to hypermedia; and animations, images, and video clips were added to better explain difficult procedures.

Since the user interface resembled the paper-based technical procedures, the new service document was immediately familiar to the technician. No additional training was required. The number of updates per year remained unchanged. However, as we will see, the cost of preparing and shipping the updates changed dramatically.

Analytical Assumptions

❏ The analysis is limited to the media conversion costs and savings associated with the original conversion from a paper-based to a CD-based system.

❏ No incremental costs were assessed for making Service Source available to Apple employees on existing servers.

❏ All current system costs are fully recovered through subscription fees paid by independent organizations that service Apple computer and peripheral products.

❏ Although Service Source has the potential to reduce training costs and enhance the productivity of field technicians, these costs are not included in the analysis.

❏ The analysis does not include any costs incurred by the service organizations for hardware/software upgrades needed to support Service Source CDs.

❏ Since there is no revenue component, the analysis does not include taxes.

Business Objectives

The original overall objectives were to enhance customer service and to reduce the cost of providing the maintenance manual content to field technicians. Based on feedback from the field and on Apple's shift to performance support systems, more recent efforts have been directed at providing all of the information and know-how needed by technicians to diagnose and repair equipment based on warranty and service contract information and to order the parts.

Determine Benefits

The benefits associated with the implementation of the CD-based Service Source program included the following:

❏ Reduced material, production, storage, and shipping and handling costs were realized.

❏ Field technicians no longer needed to spend time updating the 20-volume maintenance manual 10 times per year.

❏ Improved customer service resulted since technicians had all of the information needed to diagnose and repair computer and peripheral products.

❏ Service turnaround time was reduced, enabling technicians to handle more repairs and reduce the backlog.

❏ The quality and presentation of the information was such that less training was needed to ensure high-quality service.

❑ Fewer "no-fault found" components were returned to the factory.

❑ Technicians can take the final tests associated with Service Training's follow-up curriculum as and when needed in the field.

Service Source provides significant value to Apple and to service organizations on a demand basis because all of the information and know-how needed by a technician is available when and where it is needed. Improved customer service can improve the relationship Apple enjoys with its customers, which will lead to more orders and revenue over the long haul. However, the only quantifiable benefit used to justify the project was the reduced costs achieved by moving from the paper-based maintenance manual to an electronic hypermedia manual.

Cash Inflows

The cost of materials and production for the paper-based maintenance manuals was $110,000 per update. The total cost of preparing Service Source was $15,750 per update for the CD version, which is equivalent to $3.50 per CD for 4,500 copies. The net production savings were $94,250 per update or $942,500 per year (for 10 updates). These savings are shown in Table 3–2.

Shipping costs per update were reduced from $50,000 to $6,500 per update. Thus net savings were $43,500 per update or $435,000 per year. On an annual basis, the total savings amounted to $1,378,000.

Although the space requirements to produce, collate, assemble, and store the paper-based manuals were reduced almost to zero, this cost reduction was not included in the analysis.

Cash Outflows

The cost of converting the material from paper to digital form and rewriting the manuals to take full advantage of the interactive media environment was $1,500,000. The conversion

	Year				
	1	**2**	**3**	**4**	**Total**
Cash Inflow	($000)				
Reduced production costs	$943	$990	$1,039	$1,091	$4,062
Reduced shipping costs	$435	$457	$480	$504	$1,875
Projected cash inflow	$1,378	$1,446	$1,519	$1,595	$5,937
Cash Outflow	($000)				
Software development	$1,500	$0	$0	$0	$1,500
Media conversion	$1,500	$0	$0	$0	$1,500
Software enhancements	$0	$150	$158	$165	$473
Maintenance	$100	$105	$110	$116	$431
Total cash outflow	$3,100	$255	$268	$281	$3,904
Net cash flow	($1,723)	$1,191	$1,251	$1,313	$2,033
Cumulative cash flow	($1,723)	($531)	$720	$2,033	

Table 3–2. Detailed cash inflows (or benefits) and outflows (expenses) for Service Source

costs were considered capital costs and were depreciated over a four-year period. After the first year, all of the contributors to Service Source provided their information in digitized form, so additional conversion costs were not incurred. Conversion costs were a one-time investment since the process was shifted from paper to electronic form.

In addition, the company spent $1,500,000 on customized software development. The ongoing cost for maintenance was $100,000 per year, growing at 5 percent per year, and $150,000 for software enhancements beginning in the second year.

Table 3–2 shows the projected four-year cash flow for the program. All figures are in thousands of dollars. The total benefits or cash inflows for the first year are $1,378,000 against expenses or cash outflows of $3,100,000. Most of the expenses can be depreciated so that the profit and loss are positive in the ROI analysis. (Negative numbers are shown in parentheses.)

Most of the costs of implementing Service Source can be considered capital expenses and spread out over four years. The effect of depreciating the software and conversion costs is shown in Table 3–3. The costs to be depreciated are shown in parentheses. The effect of depreciating capital expenses reduced the overall costs on the balance sheet from $3,100,000 to $850,000 in the first year.

Cash Flow Analysis—Return on Investment

Table 3–4 summarizes the annual operating results from the original investment in Service Source. Although improved customer service invariably leads to increased sales, no attempt was made to include sales revenue in this calculation. The ROI was calculated as follows. The annual profit-and-loss (P&L) impact of $528,000 is determined by subtracting the depreciated cost of $850,000 from the cash inflow of $1,378,000. The ROI of 62 percent for the first year was calculated by dividing the first-year profit-and-loss impact of $528,000 by the depreciated cost for the first year of $850,000.

This is a facsimile of the calculation that might have been done by Apple Computer when Service Source was originally approved.

These impressive results are all pretax and are conservative, since other factors could have been included such as increased customer satisfaction resulting from better-informed service technicians. However, this illustrates the efficacy of moving from a paper- to a CD-based maintenance manual. Other measures could have been used to determine the improvement in customer service and the reduction in training needed by field technicians.

At some point in the future, systems such as Service Source may rely completely on intranets for delivery of digitized

		Depreciated Costs in Detail ($000)			
Capital Investments		1	2	3	4
Year 1	($3,100)	$750	$750	$750	$750
Year 2	($0)		$0	$0	$0
Year 3	($0)			$0	$0
Year 4	($0)				$0
Other Expenses (not depreciated)					
Maintenance		$100	$105	$110	$116
Enhancements		$0	$150	$158	$165
Total cost (depreciated)		$850	$1,005	$1,018	$1,031

Table 3–3. Apple's conversion cost from printed service manuals to multimedia. Depreciation reduces the impact of software and conversion expenditures.

	Year				
	1	2	3	4	Total
Return on investment	($000)				
Projected cash inflow	$1,378	$1,446	$1,519	$1,595	$5,937
Project cost (depreciated)	$850	$1,005	$1,018	$1,031	$3,904
Annual P&L impact	$528	$441	$501	$564	$2,033
Cumulative P&L impact	$528	$969	$1,470	$2,033	
Cumulative ROI (%) (P&L cost)	62%	96%	144%	197%	

Table 3–4. Cumulative rate of return over four years for Service Source

content. However, it is not effective to use current network services to deliver a few hundred megabytes. Intranets can be used to download files up to 1 MB in size. It is likely for at least the next few years that CD-ROM technology will continue to be used for delivery of hundreds of megabytes.

Lam Research Corporation

Lam Research Corporation is one of the world's leading suppliers of semiconductor processing equipment used to manufacture integrated circuits or semiconductor chips. Lam's technology focuses on etching and deposition. The deposition process uses complex chemical reactions that deposit *ultrapure* films on the surface of a silicon wafer. The etch process selectively removes portions of these films. These steps are repeated many times to create the semiconductor devices that are driving the technology explosion we are witnessing in all aspects of our lives.

The failure of any piece of etch or deposition equipment shuts down the wafer fabrication (fab) process since it is a serial process, which represents potential lost revenue to Lam's customers. Although Lam takes special care to design and build products that are extremely reliable, complex equipment always needs to be properly maintained and, on occasion, repaired. Lam has made a special commitment to continuously improve customer support and service.

Semiconductor manufacturing facilities must maintain extremely high levels of cleanliness. The operators of these facilities make every effort to ensure that contamination is prevented from entering deposition and etch equipment "cleanrooms." This presents special problems to the individuals who need to maintain and repair this complex equipment since ordinary paper cannot be allowed in these manufacturing facilities.

Lam had to find a solution that would provide the information needed by its own technicians and those of its customers while they work in cleanrooms.

Interactive Maintenance System

Lam developed the Interactive Maintenance System (IMS), an electronic documentation system, specifically for cleanroom use. IMS software documentation provides rapid access to assembly drawings and information, maintenance schedules and procedures, alignment and calibration procedures, and electrical schematics and wiring diagrams.

Prior to the availability of IMS, fab managers had several options, none of which was particularly effective. Engineers and technicians had to leave the cleanroom every time they needed to consult a manual, or a colleague would hold a copy of the manual against the cleanroom window so they could read it. Some fab managers had the maintenance manual laminated so that individual pages could be carried into the cleanroom. No doubt it was very frustrating for all concerned since it made maintenance and repair operations much more difficult.

IMS software is delivered over existing LANs or on a CD-ROM so it can be used on notebook computers in cleanroom environments. The user interface makes it easy for technicians and engineers to scroll through the on-line system, moving from assembly drawing to schematic, signal list, procedures, etc. The user can pan and zoom to make it easy to determine where each part is located. All of the major assemblies of single-chamber etch process equipment are shown in Figure 3–4. By clicking on the "hot buttons" along the left side of the screen, technicians can gain access to other resources on the CD-ROM.

Field personnel can go down to whatever level of detail is needed to effect a solution—simply by clicking on the appropriate assembly. In Figure 3–5, the technician accessed an annotated drawing of the harmonic arm drive assembly and a parts list.

Troubleshooting drawings are created by technicians in manufacturing for use in the field. Field personnel can tile and zoom in on drawings that are resolution sensitive. Bi-directional links make it easy to move from part number lists to drawings and back.

Hypertext links let users jump from one area of the manual to another in order to obtain all of the information related to a specific topic. Preventative maintenance (PM) procedures include links to drawings, bills of materials, and step-by-step video clips to ensure proper execution. In Figure 3 6, the step-by-step procedures include a video clip to help with a

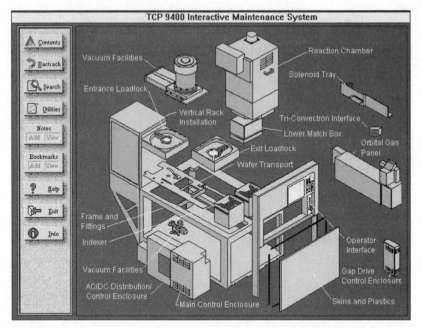

Figure 3–4. Clicking on any of the major assemblies in the exploded diagram of the etch equipment leads to more detailed information. *Source: Lam Research, Fremont, CA*

complex operation. Technicians can add bookmarks to a specific procedure to make it easier to find and add notes.

The system supports full text searches by part numbers, words, or phrases, either individually or in combination. On-line help is available so that new users can operate at a level which formerly required years of experience.

In 1995, Lam introduced Fast Access to Critical Solutions (FACS™), an electronic documentation system that is also available to customers on CD-ROM. FACS allows customers to create a customized reference library of technical information on Lam equipment. It includes troubleshooting and diagnostic information, maintenance and troubleshooting procedures, drawings and schematics, upgrade information, and best practices.

In addition, FACS includes historical information about Lam's plasma etch machines. Thus customers can have rapid access to tools and information in their cleanrooms.

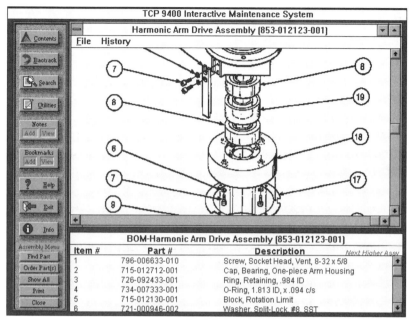

Figure 3–5. An exploded view shows how to assemble the harmonic arm drive assembly. *Source: Lam Research, Fremont, CA*

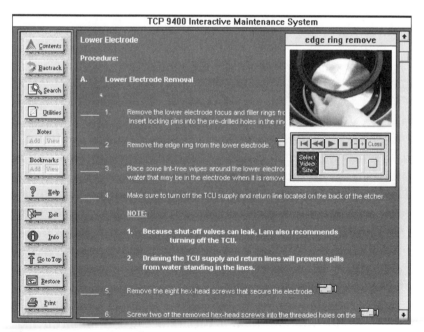

Figure 3–6. Video clips are used to augment the removal instructions for the edge ring. *Source: LAM Research, Fremont, CA*

Justification

There was no formal financial justification for development of IMS or FACS. The company believed that customer satisfaction was mandatory and that the best solution was an electronic documentation system that could be used in cleanrooms by Lam or customer technicians.

Dick Franks, manager of service technology at Lam Research Corporation, notes that technicians report productivity improvements of 5 to 10 percent, which translate into savings of $3 to $4 million per year in field service costs. These savings do not include reduced printing costs. In addition, the use of IMS has improved the mean time to repair (MTTR) and reduced unscheduled downtime, both of which are extremely important to customers.

The future holds the promise of significant improvements, including the use of multifunction virtual reality technology to show how to assemble products, which will be valuable in both the production and field service processes. Animation will also be used to clarify how the system actually works, since many operations are hidden from view on the equipment itself.

Presentation-Centric Case Studies

More attention has been paid to interactive media training case studies than any other interactive media application, so there are many good examples available in the literature. The StorageTek case study compares lecture/lab training costs with a combination of computer-based and lecture/lab training for field technicians (Hall, 1995). As you will see, it is evident that the cost savings will be much larger as lecture/lab training is discontinued for the course in question.

The Price Waterhouse study compares a computer-based training program for audit and business advisory staff with a traditional lecture/lab training program. The potential savings for this program over a five-year period approach $10 million (Hall, 1995).

In both cases, the move from traditional to interactive media training was justified solely on cost savings. No attempt was made to include gains in productivity or improvements in customer satisfaction.

StorageTek Case Study

Situation

Storage Technology Corp. (StorageTek) is the world's largest corporation focused solely on managing information storage throughout an enterprise. The company provides its customers with the ability to store, retrieve, and transmit information across networks that link everything from desktop computers to supercomputers.

In March 1995, StorageTek merged with Network Systems Corp. It was the first merger between a major enterprise storage provider and a leader in high-performance computer networking.

StorageTek customers are primarily from the Fortune 1000, the government, public sectors, and comparable international enterprises. In 1996, the company had revenues of $2.04 billion and net income of $180.3 million. Total revenues increased 6 percent in 1996 compared to 1995, principally as the result of an increase in product sales.

The company's three principal product lines are serial-access storage subsystems, random-access storage subsystems, and midrange computer products. Serial-access storage subsystems include magnetic tape storage devices and automated library systems. Random-access storage subsystem products currently consist of rotating magnetic disk devices, both in fault-tolerant Redundant Arrays of Inexpensive Disks (RAID) and non-redundant configurations, and solid-state direct-access storage devices (DASD). Midrange computer products include serial access, random access, and other products for IBM AS/400 and other midrange computer systems. StorageTek also offers software and network communication products that expand applications for its library and random-access products for efficient storage management and access. StorageTek maintains a worldwide customer support network to install, maintain, and service its own and third-party equipment.

StorageTek products and services are sold primarily through the StorageTek worldwide field force and the Network Systems Corp. worldwide field force. In addition, StorageTek products are offered through distributors in some areas, such as the Middle East and Latin America, and through remarketing agreements with companies such as Unisys Corp. and Groupe Bull.

Computer-Based Training (CBT) for Field Technicians

The company has 1,500 field technicians who provide technical support to customers around the world. In the past, training on new equipment was provided using lecture/lab format training sessions in Colorado. The technicians attended four- to ten-day sessions consisting of classroom lectures and hands-on training with the actual equipment to practice the diagnostic and repair procedures (Hall, 1995).

In 1992, the company began converting to interactive media training so technicians could be trained in their offices. The training program provides a full simulation of the equipment on a dedicated training platform (Macintosh Quadra 800 computers with 20 MB of RAM, a 17-inch monitor, and a CD-ROM drive). The courses are delivered on CD-ROMs. The files on the CD-ROM are locked to protect confidential and proprietary information. To access the training program, technicians must have the corresponding software key on the hard drive of the computer.

The technicians can view the maintenance panel of the target equipment, run diagnostics, and witness failures. Repairs are effected by selecting pictures of replacement parts and dragging them to the appropriate location on the screen to simulate replacement.

The project was justified through expense reduction rather than return on investment. Substantial savings resulted from two factors: compression of training time and reduction in travel expenses. Development and delivery of a training program was reduced from $3,291,327 for lecture/lab format to $1,748,327 for interactive media training over a three-year period.

Cost Analysis

The analysis that follows is based on a training cost model designed to identify the costs of existing training programs, to project the costs of new programs, and to contrast the costs of the two methods (lecture/lab and interactive media) of delivering training courses.

The first step was to determine the basic costs, shown in Table 3–5, which were used throughout the analysis.

The analysis was based on replacing four days of lecture/lab training with 11.2 hours of interactive media training. The interactive media training courses were to be taken at the employee's workplace.

Each of the costs listed in Table 3–6 was established using the basic costs and the number of students that were trained each year.

Table 3–5. Basic cost factors need to be gathered as they are used throughout the analysis.

Basic Costs
Expected course life
Course length
Number of students in each class
Number of times the course is held
Geographic location of the course
Average annual salaries
Fringe benefits percentage
Annual productive days
Average travel and per diem expenses
Number of instructors per class
Opportunity costs (lost sales)
Production and materials cost
Development and evaluation time

Item	Factors
Student costs	Salaries + fringe benefits + productive days + per diem + travel + opportunity (sales lost)
Instructor costs	Salaries + fringe benefits + productive days + per diem + travel
Instructional development costs	Personnel + production + materials + evaluation
Facilities costs	Annual facilities costs multiplied by course allocation
Maintenance costs	Administrative + consumable materials + revision factor

Table 3–6. Cost factors associated with the development and delivery of the training courses

Cost Comparison

The most significant costs in training are student costs. Often they represent more than 80 percent of the costs of a training program. As a result, changes in course length and/or duration have a significant effect on training costs. StorageTek chose to ignore student salaries to ensure that the results of the analysis were conservative.

Stephen Ball, training manager for the training technologies group, noted that costs savings were substantial because of reduced travel costs and training time. Training time was reduced by 60 percent when a course was converted from lecture/lab to interactive media training. The reduction was attributed to:

❑ Tighter instructional design

❑ Users being able to test out of sections

❑ Varied instructional modes: text, animation, simulation, etc., which allowed the student to learn faster and better

Table 3–7 provides the basic costs for lecture/lab and interactive media training courses.

Cost Element	Year 1	Year 2	Year 3
Number of students	200	480	250
Average travel cost	$750	$788	$827
Training days (lecture lab)	4	4	4
Per diem and car rental (lecture lab)	$65	$68	$72
Loaded labor rate for instructors and instructional designers [1]	$60	$63	$66.15
Development hours per lecture lab instructional hour	55		
Instructor costs for development of lecture lab course	$55,000	$57,750	$60,638
	$150,000	$150,000	$150,000

[1]Includes all administrative expenses for the training department, divided by the total number of hours of direct productive work by instructors and instructional designers
[2]Internal charge for depreciation of four machines used for lecture/lab training

Table 3–7. Basic costs for lecture/lab training

Some students continued to take the lecture/lab course during the transition, as shown in Table 3–8. As a result, the basic costs for interactive media must include the costs for those students who took the lecture/lab course during all three years.

The spreadsheet in Table 3–9 was prepared by StorageTek to compare costs of lecture/lab and interactive media training over a three-year period. Although the lecture/lab course length was four days, the cost comparison between the two options—four days of lecture/lab training and 11.2 hours (60 percent reduction in hours) for interactive media training plus four days of lecture/lab training for some students—is based on actual costs.

The total costs over the three years for development and delivery of a course were $1,941,320 for lecture/lab and $1,205,395 for interactive media. The net savings over the three-year period were $735,925 for an internal rate of return of 329 percent and a 15-month payback. The cost and savings

Cost Element	Year 1	Year 2	Year 3
Number of students for interactive media	200	480	250
Number of students for lecture/lab	60	96	25
Average travel cost	$750	$788	$827
Training days (lecture lab)	4	4	4
Training hours (interactive media)	11.2	11.2	11.2
Per diem and car rental	$65	$68	$72
Loaded labor rate for instructors and instructional designers	$60	$63	$66.15
Development hours per lecture lab instructional hour	55		
Instructor costs for development of lecture lab course	$55,000	$57,750	$60,638
Lab equipment costs (one machine)	$37,500	$37,500	$37,500
Training hours for interactive media course	11.2	11.2	11.2
Development hours per interactive media instructional hour	550		
Platform costs per diploma [1]	$150	$150	$150

[1] Prorated costs of the Macintosh hardware used to deliver the interactive media course

Table 3–8. Basic costs for interactive media and lecture/lab training

pattern is similar to that found in other organizations: development costs for interactive media courses tend to be higher, but delivery costs are lower when compared to lecture/lab courses.

Price Waterhouse Case Study

Situation

Price Waterhouse provides audit, tax, accounting, and business consulting services to customers around the world. The company's services encompass accounting, auditing, tax

| | Lecture/Lab Training | | | Interactive Media and Lecture/Lab | | |
| | Year | | | Year | | |
Cost Elements	1	2	3	1	2	3
Travel and living costs	$215,000	$541,800	$296,750	$64,500	$108,360	$29,630
Instructor costs	$55,000	$115,500	$121,275	$55,000	$57,750	$60,638
Classroom costs	$6,600	$13,860	$14,553	$6,600	$6,930	$7,277
Development and maint. costs[1]	$92,400	$9,240	$9,702	$462,000	$48,510	$46,200
Interactive media platform costs	N/A	N/A	N/A	$30,000	$72,000	$37,500
Lab equipment	$150,000	$150,000	$150,000	$37,500	$37,500	$37,500
Total costs	$519,000	$830,400	$592,280	$655,600	$328,740	$221,054
Difference (lecture/lab minus interactive media)				($136,600)	$498,990	$373,535

[1]Interactive media course development costs include the cost of the lecture/lab course development on which the interactive media course is based.

Table 3–9. Time and money saved by moving from lecture/lab to interactive media training

planning and compliance, strategic management consulting, information technology, and many disciplines within these categories. Price Waterhouse has locations in over 100 countries and employs more than 53,000 people.

Computer-Based Training

Price Waterhouse created a CBT program called Terminal RISK to train its professional audit staff. It is part of a worldwide training initiative designed to support the company's business strategy. As part of the core training for all Audit

and Business Advisory Staff (ABS), the Terminal RISK provides instruction in computerized information systems. The
course is taken during the third year of training of audit staff,
and it is a prerequisite for a week-long residential classroom
course (Hall, 1995).

The company report detailing the project indicates that
there is an important job performance need in the ABS business sector because clients of various sizes in a variety of
industries increasingly rely on information produced by computerized information systems. ABS staff must be able to:

1. Adopt management's perspective on such systems,
   i.e., view them for their contribution to the business
   and not simply as an audit problem

2. Understand the implications of such systems at a
   practical level for both the audit process and the
   business as a whole

The development of the program was driven by two factors: it was a business-critical subject and accomplished
instructors were not available. Instructor-led training in this
subject area is difficult, because it demands both deep technical knowledge and instructional skills to make a complex
subject interesting.

Cost Analysis

The training program has been taken by more than 7,000
employees in 50 countries. To determine the benefits of the
CBT course, Price Waterhouse conducted a training effectiveness review. Compared to traditional classroom training, the
CBT course reduced by 50 percent the time needed for
learners to attain the same standard of knowledge. Total
costs for development and delivery over a five-year period
were examined.

The training effectiveness review included a ROI analysis
for the program. Results indicated that the cost per student
was substantially reduced with interactive media training
when compared to instructor-led. The cost of developing and
implementing the Terminal RISK program was $1,600,000.

Instructor-Led Training Expense Item	Cost per Student
Extra day of student time (7 hours at $50 per hour)	$350
Instructor time (14 hours at $250)	$140
Travel and accommodation	$250
Facility costs	$20
Total cost per student	$760

Table 3–10. Costs of implementing instructor-led training for Price Waterhouse's ABS (Audit and Business Advisory Staff) training

Overall development costs were $750,000 and implementation costs were $850,000. The net cost per student, based on an average of 3,000 students per year and a program shelf life of five years, was $106 per student. This was calculated by dividing the total cost by the number of students who would take the course over the life of the course.

The estimated costs of implementing an instructor-led equivalent are shown in Table 3–10. Class size was assumed to be 25 students.

Thus the total cost for instructor-led training for 3,000 students was $2,280,000 for the first year.

Price Waterhouse implemented the CBT course on a widespread basis and expected to achieve total savings of approximately $10 million (when compared to instructor-led training) by the end of 1995. The savings were calculated by multiplying the savings per student ($760 minus $106) times 3,000 students per year times five years. In addition, the company generated incremental revenue through the sale of the Terminal RISK course to other organizations.

The non-financial benefits of the program include:

❑ Consistent, high-quality training on a worldwide basis

❑ Engaging and appealing treatment of a subject for which students had little affinity

❑ The self-paced nature of the course proved to be valuable since the ABS staff have a wide range of experience, background, and seniority

Price Waterhouse attributes the success of the program to the following:

❏ The project appraisal focused on the needs of the business
❏ Strong support from the organization leadership
❏ Full integration with the internal training program
❏ Company commitment to the appropriate use of technology
❏ Global focus, leading to substantial impact on a highly decentralized business
❏ Excellent economics because of the audience

REFERENCES

Hall, Brandon. 1995. Return-on-investment and multimedia training. *Multimedia Training Newsletter* and Macromedia, Inc.

Fetterman, Roger L., and Byrne, H. Richard. 1995. *Interactive Selling in the '90s.* San Diego: Ellipsys International Publications.

Fetterman, Roger L., and Gupta, Satish K. 1995. *Mainstream Multimedia.* New York: Van Nostrand Reinhold.

4

Planning and Analysis—The Basis for Success

At the beginning of this book, I set the stage for interactive media as the wave of the future—allowing businesses to fully exploit the "hidden gold" of corporate information and knowledge. The remainder of this book will focus on networked interactive media, with a single caveat: in some cases, a CD-ROM or DVD may be used to transport large interactive media files simply because the broadband network is either not available or it is too expensive for the application.

Even though businesses may be somewhat naive about the Internet and how to fully exploit it, the rapidly growing interest in networked solutions is not happening by accident. Changes in organizational emphasis from vertical structure to horizontal process dictate that sharing information and know-how and collaborating are available to self-managing teams. The shift to a global, digital economy can survive only through effective communications. And finally, computing and networking technologies enable businesses to operate in ways that were not conceivable a decade ago.

Any solutions that focus on delivering information and knowledge where, when, and how they are needed immediately lead us to performance support systems. As discussed in previous chapters, a performance support system is an electronic system that provides integrated, on-demand access to information, advice, learning experiences, and tools to enable a high level of job performance with a minimum of support from other people.

Performance support systems, combined with the ability to share information and knowledge and to collaborate with individuals, teams, partners, and customers, are the key to mining the hidden gold of interactive media. The planning process that follows was explicitly designed to serve individuals who want to apply networked interactive media in support of business processes.

The Interactive Media Planning Process

The multi-step methodology that follows is appropriate for the application of any type of technology to business processes. It provides a step-by-step approach that reinforces the need to understand the mission and processes of the corporation, to establish measurable results, to apply technologies in concert with corporate goals, and finally to determine the payback of the investment.

1. Review the overall goals and objectives of the corporation
2. Establish a measurable set of goals for the selected process
3. Model the selected process and develop a complete set of metrics
4. Select technologies that enhance the process
5. Perform ROI analysis to establish the payback

Corporate Goals and Objectives

Before embarking on major networked interactive media investment programs, it is appropriate to review recent shifts in the business environment. The actions of competitors or the opening up of new market opportunities may present an opportunity to revector primary goals or objectives.

Many companies are partnering in new ways that fundamentally shift the way business is being conducted. Even though you may plan to continue to manufacture and distribute your line of products, you could choose to partner with a qualified group of associates who design, develop, produce, and deliver many of the components you need on a just-in-time basis. In this case, your overall goals and objective could change significantly even though you are still in the same line of business.

The important point is to ensure that the project team is fully aware of corporate goals because they will help you make good decisions during the planning process.

Measurable/Realizable Goals

The starting point for the creation of a worthwhile interactive media application is the development of a set of measurable and realizable business goals for the business process in question. These process-specific goals must be consistent with corporate goals and objectives.

A primary goal in for-profit businesses is to increase profits. Profits increase shareholder value and dividends. Profits allow corporations to invest in the development of new products and services. If profits do not increase, the business suffers along with its ability to grow and invest.

Companies usually have other goals and objectives, such as:

- ❏ Improve customer service
- ❏ Enter and dominate a new market segment
- ❏ Increase revenue
- ❏ Increase profitability

- ❏ Improve performance and productivity
- ❏ Improve product quality
- ❏ Increase velocity to market of new products and services
- ❏ Establish a strong corporate position in the market

The important point is to establish *measurable* goals and objectives for the selected process that are in line with the overall goals of the corporation. Technology projects that are not aligned with business goals are likely to fail.

The goals become the benchmarks for measuring success for both employees and managers. However, the goals may be quite different for the individual stakeholders. Senior business managers are rewarded for achieving corporate goals. Employees are rewarded for achieving process goals, and in some cases for their contribution to corporate goals.

An examination of any business process will reveal that multiple types of capabilities may be needed to satisfy the needs of the process. For example, engineers who are collaborating on the design of a complex product might need, in addition to three-dimensional design tools, desktop video-conferencing with screen- and file-sharing capability over a high-speed interactive media network. Tellers at a bank might need access to the knowledge base of the bank in addition to just-in-time learning modules and account information simultaneously when dealing with a customer. An electronic catalog that includes configuration rules and up-to-date pricing might satisfy the needs of sales representatives when they visit their clients.

Interactive media capabilities may not play a role in all elements of the business, but where they do they can have a dramatic impact. Indeed, the contribution of interactive media may be so important that it becomes the driving force for the project.

Modeling the Process

A model of the target process is fundamental to understanding all of the stages of the process and the activities within each stage. A model ensures that all of the groups involved will be able to communicate effectively because it is based on a common understanding of the process.

A flow chart of the process can be invaluable as it will help identify all the corresponding tasks and serve as a blueprint for efforts to apply networked interactive and other capabilities. Further, the process model can be used to identify all of the individuals and groups that are part of the process. This is important since processes tend to be horizontal and cross the vertical, organizational boundaries of the corporation. And finally, it can be used to determine candidate activities for investments and to establish the potential value of the investments.

Each of the six steps will be explained in detail below.

1. Establish the overall return-on-investment metrics
2. Model the selected business process (or processes) and break it into its component parts (e.g., phases, steps, tasks, etc.)
3. Establish metrics for each task (cost, resources, and time)
4. Determine the value of each component in terms of process/corporate goals
5. Establish the overall metrics of the process
6. Consult with multiple sources to assess the value of individual activities

Armed with the flow chart and a set of business goals, the project team will be able to determine the steps that can benefit from the application of interactive media, groupware, collaborative computing, desktop videoconferencing, and other sets of capabilities. This type of analysis automatically places interactive media capabilities in a business context since they'll be applied to satisfy some or all of the needs of a particular business process.

Overall ROI Metrics

The overall cost of the process must be understood along with the value of the outputs of the process. The cost is the investment and the output is the return on that investment. This provides the baseline metrics of the process. In the sales process, the investment is the total amount spent to generate sales and the output is the total sales revenue.

The metrics of other processes may be more difficult to establish, but it is important to establish this overall view of the process. It provides the perspective needed to understand the process in the overall operation of the business.

When interactive media capabilities become an integral part of an overall solution based on computing and networking technologies, their value can be linked directly to business processes that corporations understand. The establishment of measures provides the foundation for determining the cost of each activity in a business process (time, money, and resources) and for demonstrating the value of the activity to process and business goals.

Process Models and Component Parts

By way of illustration, a typical sales process for sophisticated computer or networking products is shown in Table 4–1. Specific models are shown for each of the business processes discussed in the book.

A flow chart for this process might look like the sequence depicted in Figure 4–1. The flow chart will vary according to the activities or tasks that are pertinent to a specific sale so the activities or tasks in each stage will not necessarily be the same for each situation.

Prospecting	Qualifying	Developing	Closing
Cold calls	Send literature	Create proposal and/or presentation	Fine-tune proposal
Direct mail	Qualify by phone	Visit client to demo/propose	Quote delivery and availability
Seminars	Make appointments	Respond to questions and objections	Sign contract
Referrals	Send demo or sample	Get pricing approval	Collect money
Advertising	Follow-up activities	Follow-up activities	Follow-up activities

Table 4–1. A typical sales process comprises multiple activities.

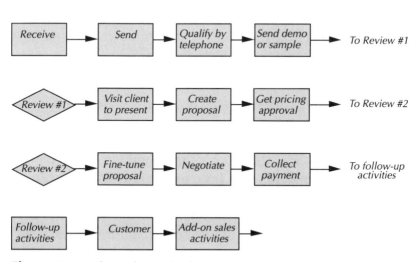

Figure 4–1. Flow chart of sales activities related to a specific sale

Establishing Activity/Task Metrics

At this point, all of the activities have been identified, so it is possible to establish the metrics (i.e., time, money, and resources) for each activity or task. How long does it take to accomplish the task in the current environment and who needs to be involved? A timeline can be prepared for each activity or task to help pinpoint where the process gets bogged down.

For example, in the sales process example, the timelines might indicate that the proposal preparation and approval process are consuming far too much time in the overall sales cycle. In a customer service environment, the time taken to retrieve up-to-date account information may be too long compared to your competitors. In a product development process, the time needed to set up and conduct review meetings after each major step may be the reason that the corporation cannot achieve the desired velocity to market.

By determining the metrics, we have a baseline that we can use for comparison with the networked interactive media solution.

The Value of Activities

The individuals and groups that participate in the process are likely to be the best candidates for determining the value of each activity or task. This step should identify the critical success factors in the process that deliver a satisfactory result. These factors should be the first ones to examine when looking at the attributes of the computer and communications technologies and the content that is available for use in the process. For example, in the sales process example, a knowledge base and configurator that allow the sales rep to prepare quotations on the spot might be a critical success factor.

Selecting the Right Technologies

In the previous step, we gathered inputs from various individuals that will help us ascertain which activities would benefit from the availability of corporate know-how and up-to-date information—from access to an electronic product catalog or an interactive media instruction sheet for setting up production equipment or just-in-time learning modules and from the availability of collaborative computing and desktop videoconferencing equipment.

To understand the process, list each of the available technologies and describe the attributes and benefits of each. Match the attributes and benefits first with the critical success factors and then with all other activities and tasks as shown in Figure 4–2.

The process depicted in Figure 4–3 can be used to match the attributes/benefits offered by the capabilities of software products with individual activities in business processes. Determining when and how they are used is dictated by their value in fulfilling the goals of the business process.

If sales reps need to be able to configure products or systems while meeting with prospective customers, a notebook computer with an electronic product catalog and configuration and quotation tools may be critical to success. If expert support is needed, then remote access to an intranet site with appropriate repositories may be another critical part of the solution.

The value of each set of capabilities is assessed by using the business and process filters to determine if the specific set helps employees to be more effective at achieving the goals of the specific process. For example, how well do the attributes of client/server technology fit the "corporate goals" and the critical success factors established for an intranet application for field service personnel? How well do the attributes of personal productivity tools fit the corporate goals for greater profitability and sales process goals for increased revenue and improved customer service?

If high-impact, customized presentations are critical to getting the order, presentations derived from the information stored in an interactive media database should be considered. The interactive media database can also be used as the basis for learning modules if product and industry knowledge is important to the success of individual tasks in the process and the overall process itself.

Available Technologies, Tools, and Capabilities

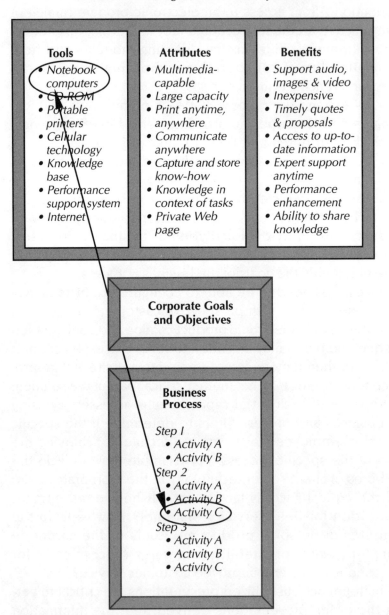

Figure 4–2. Matching the attributes of the technologies with critical success factors and sales activities

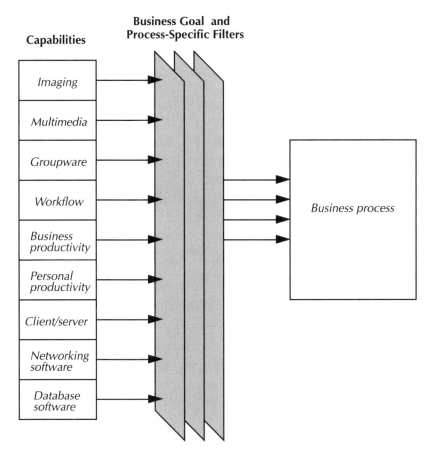

Figure 4–3. A model for applying software capabilities to business processes

The methodology for understanding business processes and the application of capabilities to the processes will be discussed in each of the case studies in Chapters 5 through 7. For the moment, we have established a new way of looking at applications, capabilities, and business processes that will yield measurable results which satisfy individual employees, business processes, and business goals.

The Final Step

Organizations that understand their business processes at the level of depth described above are in an ideal position. They can go beyond using technology simply to automate the old ways of doing business to taking advantage of technology for changing the nature of the work. These organizations involve their suppliers in the design of their products (e.g., Boeing involving its suppliers in the design of the 777), or become information providers to their customers (e.g., Bergen Brunswig providing its knowledge base to druggists so they can make better business decisions when buying products), or deliver products that are customized for the buyer (e.g., Chrysler delivering an automobile based on the specifications a customer input into a kiosk at the dealer's showroom).

Most of the processes described in this book begin and end with customers. Networked interactive media enable a corporation to develop entirely new relationships with customers which can lead to sustainable competitive advantage—something that superior products may no longer be able to provide in this fast-paced world.

The Bottom Line for Interactive Media

Corporations use return on investment (ROI) analysis to compare the dollars invested in a project to the dollars returned. In the final analysis, the evaluation must deal with the impact of interactive media solutions on the operation of the business. ROI analysis determines what the project will contribute to the bottom line.

In addition, ROI spreadsheets can be used for sensitivity analysis. By varying the potential cash inflows and outflows, you will be able to develop a thorough understanding of the dynamics of a proposed sales automation or customer service system, or a system for just-in-time delivery of information and learning modules on the factory floor, or any other interactive media system. Both the upside potential of the project and the downside risk can be evaluated to help convince senior management of the merits of the project.

ROI models can be used for cost/benefit analysis to support decision-making activities (e.g., spending money on sales force automation or on manufacturing improvements) or for cost-effectiveness analysis to compare different ways of carrying out the same objective (e.g., interactive training or performance support systems).

In some cases, ROI analysis is viewed by project managers as an accounting exercise that is to be avoided unless demanded by management. Even if management doesn't demand it, ROI analysis should be part of every interactive media project. It introduces a rigor into the effort that helps ensure the technologies will be applied to satisfy business needs. The multilevel ROI model described below can be used to:

- ❏ Justify the planned expenditures
- ❏ Establish all of the benefits, even those that cannot easily be quantified
- ❏ Conduct sensitivity analysis to show upside potential and downside risk
- ❏ Evaluate the effectiveness of the program after implementation

In the final analysis, ROI models serve as a benchmark against which the company can determine what worked and what didn't work. The use of interactive media capabilities in business processes is a journey—not a single event. Even though senior management may not demand a formal ROI presentation for a project, project managers owe it to themselves and the potential beneficiaries of the project to better understand the process and the results achieved. An ROI model is an excellent management tool for complex projects.

Going forward, it is important to know which of the forecasted benefits were realized and how well they were realized. Perhaps there is more to be gained by additional investments in a given area, or the investments should be made in another stage of the process altogether. ROI models should be viewed and used as a tool for making wise investments—not as a bureaucratic exercise designed to slow down the process.

Establishing Measures

Multilevel ROI models have little value unless benefits and costs can be quantified. The starting point for creating a worthwhile interactive media solution should be the development of a measurable and realizable set of business goals for the application or process.

Business goals or objectives for the sales process can include any or all of the following:

- ❏ *Increase revenue*—Increase sales through productivity improvements and maximize sales potential through improved quantification and prioritization.

- ❏ *Improve customer service*—Provide more timely response to customer queries, more accurate information about company products and services, and better access to company executives.

- ❏ *Improve products*—Reduce defects through the use of interactive media-assembly instructions or collaboration with customers during product design.

- ❏ *Increase productivity*—Reduce sales support costs by providing on-line access to corporate knowledge bases.

- ❏ *Improve velocity to market*—Ensure the sales force is fully trained at product launch by providing learning modules in advance of product announcement.

Companies may have other goals as well. For example, if a company plans to enter a new segment of the market, the objective may be to establish a dominant position in the selected niche. The Gannett Company wanted to regain market share in newspaper advertising that had been lost to competition from other media and direct mail. StorageTek wanted to reduce the cost of delivering mass-customized solutions. Val-Pak's objective was to improve the close ratio, i.e., reduce the number of cold calls per deal closed.

By definition, the objectives for projects in any of the core business processes must be realizable and measurable. Once they have been set, it is usually possible to establish the metrics needed to determine if the goals and objectives have been reached.

Constructing a Multilevel Financial Model

Most large corporations have a standard set of guidelines for evaluating capital investments. Some use payback, while others use an accounting based on return of net assets or a discounted cash flow analysis. While financial experts may argue the merits of one form of analysis over the others, the reader needs to ensure that the method approved by his or her company is used. The examples shown in the case studies are based on either a multilevel evaluation/ROI model or a discounted cash flow analysis.

The multilevel evaluation/ROI model has been used in a variety of industries for the application of interactive media capabilities in training or other applications. It is used in this book for case studies to support decision-making activities or for cost-effectiveness analysis which compares different ways to achieve an objective; for example, continuing the current lecture/lab training program versus implementing computer-based training. It is not used to analyze the merits of interactive media in the sales process where variable revenue contributions are the key benefit.

The discounted rate of return on investment approach can be found in modern financial reference books. The analyses calculate incremental cash inflows for comparison with incremental cash outflows. The balance is discounted to determine if the discounted ROI exceeds the company's average cost of capital (or the incremental cost of capital). Usually you should choose the investments that have the highest return relative to the funds available for investment.

Figure 4–4 shows the steps to be followed in constructing a multilevel financial model, using either the multilevel ROI model or the discounted rate of return approach.

Determine the Benefits

All of the possible benefits of the interactive media project should be listed under the appropriate headings—cost reduction, improved products, increased productivity, and revenue gain—and quantified where possible. Many of the benefits of interactive media projects can be quantified, but some are more direct—and therefore more credible—than others. It may not be possible to quantify other benefits, but they can be directly related to a measurable benefit.

Modeling the business process helps immeasurably since all of the activities have been identified, their contribution to the success of the process and to corporate goals has been identified, and their metrics (cost, time, and resources) have been determined. All of the elements in the process are related by the model, making it easier to rationalize the benefits to be used in the ROI process.

All of the quantifiable benefits should be ranked according to their contribution to the overall objectives of the application or process. The ranking should account for the benefits that apply directly to corporate goals or imperatives.

Quantifiable benefits that apply both to the business process and to corporate goals should be earmarked for inclusion in the ROI analysis. Such benefits will likely appeal to senior managers whose support is needed to proceed with the interactive media project. If your CEO has decided that enhanced customer service is a corporate imperative, then projects that contribute to this goal will likely be supported (assuming that they satisfy the goals of the project as well). If increased velocity to market is a corporate goal, then projects that help shorten the product design and launch cycle will be viewed with favor.

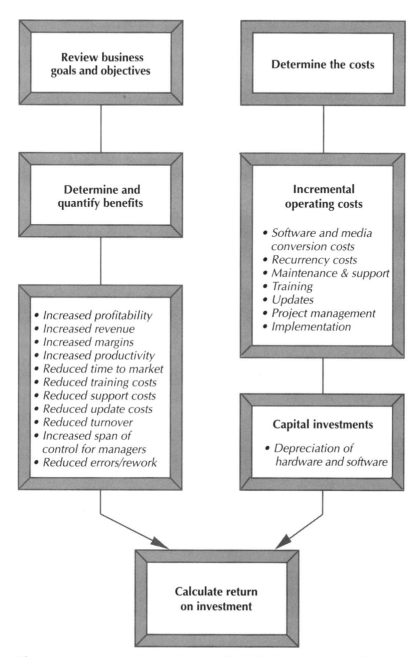

Figure 4–4. Steps for analyzing all of the factors and calculating the return on investment

The ROI analysis can be made using the top-ranked bene-fits to determine if the return will justify the proposed inter-active media program. The initial ROI model is used to demonstrate return based on top-ranked benefits. If a larger ROI is needed, other benefits can be added as necessary. It is best to justify the program by showing a return that is appropriate to the nature of the corporate culture. Most deci-sion makers look for a break-even point of two to three years for cash flow and a positive profit-and-loss in the first or sec-ond year.

A return of 50 percent is desirable and anything over 500 percent is questionable unless all of the evidence is extremely solid. However, in some cases the leverage that can be obtained may result in returns greater than 500 per-cent. For example, the preliminary results of a return-on-investment study of intranets based on Netscape technology (conducted by International Data Corporation in 1996) demonstrated typical ROIs greater than 1000 percent. Intra-net investments can result in ROIs that are much higher than usually found for technology investments.

Note that even though all of the benefits are not included in the model, it is important to track all of the benefits that can be quantified as the interactive media project is imple-mented. This provides a complete picture of the actual pro-gram's return on investment.

Quantify the Benefits

The benefits of interactive media solutions are manifested in productivity improvements, raised product quality, cost reductions, and increased revenue, as shown below.

Increased productivity   Improved training methods, hyper-media documentation, corporate knowledge bases, perfor-mance support systems, and other interactive media solutions can contribute to improvements in productivity as follows:

❑ Average time to reach equivalent levels of achieve-ment can be reduced through CBT and performance support systems.

- ❑ Opportunity costs (lost sales) are reduced since employees spend less time away from the job.
- ❑ Sales cycles are shortened for sales representatives with access to corporate knowledge bases.
- ❑ Product quality is improved using assembly instructions with interactive media elements.
- ❑ Design cycles are reduced through collaborative work environments.
- ❑ Less time is used to acquire the information needed to make decisions.
- ❑ More employees achieve mastery of learning materials.
- ❑ New products, concepts, processes, procedures, etc., can be introduced and integrated into operations more rapidly.
- ❑ Customer queries can be responded to more quickly and accurately. The use of a performance support system allowed employees of a leading manufacturer of telecommunications equipment to reduce the time and effort to respond to customer inquiries by 50 percent.

Reduced cost   Cost reductions tend to be easy to measure and flow through to the bottom line because accounting practices and measures allow us to demonstrate savings as follows:

- ❑ The cost of development, maintenance, and delivery of interactive media can be less than conventional training courses
- ❑ Cost reductions in creation, maintenance, production, and distribution of paper-based reference materials and manuals
- ❑ Reduced costs because of fewer delays and lower negative consequences resulting from delays
- ❑ Reductions in the amount of overtime at peak periods because of improved operations
- ❑ Decreased direct expenditures for training and learning, such as reduced student and instructor per diem

cost, decreased learning time, the ability to handle more students at a reduced rate per student, and improved facilities utilization

❏ Reduced customer support costs using on-line support, desktop videoconferencing, and collaborative computing

❏ Space reduction for electronic versus manual storage

❏ Reduced travel costs through CBT, EPSS, and desktop videoconferencing with collaborative computing

Increased revenue   Although it is often difficult to measure improvements in this area that directly impact the bottom line, it is clear that the revenue contribution of sales and sales support personnel will improve. Many managers disregard the benefits because they believe they would have received the order anyway. A paradigm shift may be needed before measures based on the items below can be included in ROI analysis. However, all successful sales organizations operate on the principle that sales revenues increase when more time is spent making sales calls.

❏ Increased sales because more productive time is spent in front of the customer

❏ Increased sales because the sales representatives have access to corporate knowledge bases

❏ Increased sales because products can be introduced more quickly

❏ More effective portrayal of the company products and services in the context of the prospect's business

❏ More employees operating at the level of the top performers (the performance gap between top- and middle-level performers can be reduced using EPSS)

❏ Improved service, credibility with customers, and responsiveness leads to fewer canceled orders, more referrals, and better customer loyalty

❏ Distribution channels are more effective sooner because of more rapid and effective product introductions

Determine the Costs (Incremental Operating and Capital Investment)

Most of the incremental costs in implementing performance support systems are considered capital investments. The interactive media computers selected for the users of the system, the initial acquisition cost of software, and the media conversion costs all fall into this category. In addition, it is often appropriate to include money for modifications (recurrency development) to the original material. These initial capital investments are shown as negative cash flows in period zero. Typically, the life of interactive media programs is three or four years.

Capital assets are depreciated over their useful life (i.e., the life of the program). Depreciation reduces the impact of the capital investment in the early years by spreading it out over the life of the program. Most of the examples cited below are for four-year programs, but the actual number you use should come from your financial management group.

Training, support, hardware maintenance, and project management costs are included as operating expenses that are not depreciated.

Calculate ROI

Most large companies have standard guidelines for evaluating capital investments. Some companies use payback, others use an accounting method based on return of net assets, and still others use a discounted cash flow analysis. In general, the project in question must produce a return on investment that is greater than the average cost of capital to the company.

Most of the examples that follow are based on the discounted cash flow method.[1] The theory behind the discounted cash flow analysis is that dollars received later in the project are worth less because of the time value of money. In addition, investors expect to earn a certain rate of return based on the level of risk they are willing to accept. The time value of money and the risk premium are incorporated into the discount rate.

Investments in a piece of equipment with proven cost savings will carry a much lower discount rate than a new and unproved software venture. Apple Computer's rate varies from 12 to 13 percent.

Apple Computer derives a discount rate based on the Capital Asset Pricing Model (CAPM). The company looks at the capital structure of the firm doing the financing. It derives the cost of equity and the cost of debt for the particular investment and weights them based on the capital structure of the firm.

However, it is important to remember that the method chosen must reflect the particular guidelines used by your company. It is important to work with your company's financial group to ensure that the calculations will be consistent with company practices.

The classic discounted rate of return on investment approach calculates and compares the incremental cash outflows and inflows. By discounting the balance, you can determine whether the discounted rate of return exceeds the company's cost of capital. Typically, companies choose the investments that yield the highest rate of return relative to the funds that are available for investment.

Sensitivity Analysis

ROI models can be used for sensitivity analysis. The results can be valuable when pursuing project approval. For example, in a sales automation project, what happens to the ROI if the incremental sales are less than those forecast? Does the project still satisfy company standards? Similarly, if the expenses are 25 percent greater than those forecast, what is the impact on the ROI?

Sensitivity analysis enables the company to explore the risk associated with the potential investment and helps you win the confidence of senior management.

Progressive companies that understand the value of applying technology to enhance business processes tend to evaluate new technology investments based on increased customer satisfaction, increased velocity to market for new products, product enhancement, and employee performance. The key goal is to enhance performance by providing the tools and training needed by employees on the job.

The following case study was selected because it illustrates how to apply the models and methodologies described in this chapter.

Hewlett-Packard Company Case Study

Hewlett-Packard Company designs, manufactures, and services electronic products and systems for measurement, computing, and communication; these products and systems are used by people in industry, business, engineering, science, medicine and education. HP is one of the 19 largest industrial companies in the United States and one of the world's largest computer companies. The company had revenues of $38.4 billion for the fiscal year ended October 31, 1996. Headquartered in Palo Alto, California, the company employs approximately 112,000 people, 59,000 of whom work in the United States.

The success story unfolding at Hewlett-Packard demonstrates the value of understanding the buying and selling processes and the goals and objectives of the corporation. HP's sales automation project does not yet take full advantage of networked interactive media, but it is headed in the right direction.

This example illustrates the opportunities and obstacles that organizations face when applying networked interactive media in a field sales environment. It also serves as a reminder that human resources can be used to advantage in situations where the technology is not yet feasible.

Computer Systems Organization

In 1993, the Computer Systems Organization of Hewlett-Packard embarked on a seven-year program designed to solve process and support problems for the sales force in the Americas—1,000 in the U.S. and 200 each in Canada and Latin America. The company realized that it had to make some changes because the market was growing rapidly and it wanted to improve the profitability of the computer systems organization.

Even though Hewlett-Packard is the number-two U.S.-based computer/office equipment company, its position would not be secure unless it grew faster than the market for computer systems.

HP did not go through a formal ROI analysis for project approval because the pressure to move forward was so great. Management directed the project team to "do it, and do it well." To illustrate how the company might have used the methodologies outlined in this book, I have prepared a facsimile of the return on investment analysis the company might have used.

The drivers that were forcing change in 1993 included:

❑ Sales had to grow faster than the market (>20% yearly).
❑ The sales cost per order dollar had to be reduced significantly.
❑ Sales productivity had to increase significantly.
❑ HP needed to move to new sales process models.
  ▪ Large account selling by industry
  ▪ More effective use of distribution channels

The project extends beyond sales automation and involves changing the way that HP does business with its customers now and how it will do business in the future. The company broke the project into three distinct phases over the period 1993 to 1998, each of which comprises multiple individual initiatives. The extended time period gave HP the opportunity to try various technological solutions and to reject those that did not serve the goals and objectives of the project.

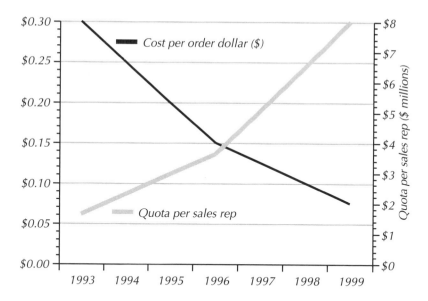

Figure 4–5. Cost of selling and sales rep productivity goals
Source: Hewlett-Packard, Palo Alto, CA

Overall return-on-investment metrics   The overall goals and objectives for the project are shown in Figure 4–5. The productivity of the sales reps needed to increase by a factor of five, and the cost per order dollar needed to decrease by a factor of four. The goals were dictated by the growth rate of the industry and the need to contain costs. They represented a considerable challenge to the Computer Systems Organization.

Model the sales process   The project team used surveys and focus groups to identify inhibitors that impacted selling effectiveness. Feedback from the sales representatives provided the following perspectives:

❑ Quota was increasing every year.
❑ There was accelerating price/performance pressure on their product line.
❑ Sales administrative support had shifted back to sales reps.

❏ Customers expected more added value from vendors.

❏ "Broken" processes added excessive non-value-added work.

❏ HP was not using its own products to advantage (the Cobbler's Children Syndrome).

To sum up, sales reps said that there is "not enough time to do all the things that the company is asking me to do."

The project team concluded that sales reps were spending 50 percent of their time on administrative work—looking for information or following up on customer queries. It was very difficult and time consuming for the sales reps to prepare configurations in response to their customers' requirements. The ability of sales reps to respond quickly with accurate configuration information is a critical factor in the sale of computer systems. Sometimes HP was not competitive because it took too long to respond to customers and prospects.

The goal of the project team was to provide easy access to information and resources so sales reps could apply them productively in the sales process and communicate with customers more effectively.

The project team determined that the final solution had to have the following attributes if it were to succeed in HP's environment.

❏ Provide immediate access to relevant information when and where it was needed by sales reps

❏ Allow sales reps to share customer and sales information and tactics

❏ Allow sales reps to configure, quote, and order most systems with acknowledgment within minutes

❏ Support customer configuration of the order and initiate the fulfillment process without HP employee involvement

Match technology benefits with activities   It was clear from the onset that HP needed to provide better information and support in a hurry. Since it would take a significant amount of time and effort to develop computer-based configuration tools, the project team decided to create configuration support teams to provide immediate relief. Over the course of the project, a configuration and quotation tool set would be provided for use on the sales reps' notebook computers.

In the short term, sales specialists were added in each sales district to handle the administrative workload and free up the sales reps. In the long term, information access, opportunity tools, and enhanced support processes will be used.

Training and support are prerequisites to success in this environment. It is not feasible to pull 1,400 sales reps out of the field for traditional classroom training. HP adopted a number of techniques including lunchroom and after-work seminars, computer-based training, and a technical mentoring system to satisfy the needs of the sales force. The company realized that it needed to establish a continuous learning environment over the course of the project. Sales reps need to learn how to use the technologies effectively to accomplish daily tasks and activities. Ultimately, learning modules will become part of an overall performance support system for the field sales force.

Figure 4–6 relates the activities in the sales process to attributes and benefits of available technologies and tools that are being used by HP employees. Sales reps need to be close to their customers so they operate out of home offices. Notebook computers that allow the sales reps to make interactive media presentations and configure and price systems are mandatory items. Up-to-date product literature had to be available on an "as needed" basis.

Each of the items that comprise the final solution were selected after the project team determined what types of capabilities were needed to satisfy the activities in each stage of the sales process.

One of the primary goals of the project was to enable the sales reps to configure and price systems in the field. Initially this need is being satisfied by expert configuration teams. In the mid-term, it will be satisfied by a portable configurator and quotation tool set on the sales rep's notebook computer.

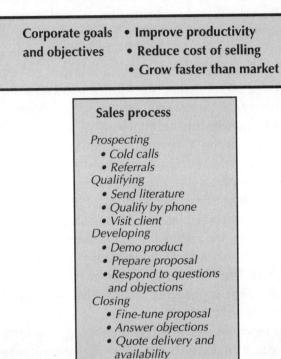

Figure 4–6. Technologies and tools linked to the sales process

In the long term, customers will also have access to the configurator and pricing information at an HP Web site.

Interactive media are becoming a more significant factor because they make presentations and learning experiences more compelling. In the short term, interactive media content will likely be delivered using CD-ROMs. Files that are smaller than 1 MB will be delivered on HP's intranet. Current networks are not cost effective for delivering hundreds of megabytes to 1,400 sales reps.

It is noteworthy that HP found a way to satisfy the needs of the sales reps in the short term which gave the company time to arrange for technology-based solutions that will carry the sales force forward in the longer term.

The following analysis is based on information provided by Hewlett-Packard and on the author's experience. The assumptions made by the author are realistic for the computer systems business but may differ from the actual numbers that HP would use. It is intended to illustrate the potential value that organizations can realize through the application of human resources and technological capabilities to business processes.

Establish the overall metrics   As noted in Figure 4–5, HP had established the current cost-per-order dollar and the productivity of each sales rep and goals for the future. The company knew that it had to grow faster than the market if it were to remain a leader in the long term. In addition, sales reps were spending more than 50 percent of their time on activities that added no value to customers. In the short and medium term (from 1993 to 1996), support resources plus early technological solutions were enabling HP to meet its goals. In the long term, networked interactive media will have significant value, since the role of the sales reps must change. This notion is explored in greater depth following the ROI calculation.

List of benefits   The list of benefits at the top of the next page can be used to justify the expenditures over the period 1993 to 1997.

❏ Cost per order dollar reduced from $0.30 to less than $0.15

❏ Sales productivity increased from $1.6 to more than $3.6 million per sales rep

❏ Increased customer satisfaction since responses are faster and more accurate

❏ Reduced documentation costs

❏ Reduced turnover since the project demonstrates management commitment to sales reps

Dick Knudsten, sales force productivity manager, notes that, as of this writing, the computer system organization has been able to meet the targets it established for cost-per-order dollar and sales productivity.

The benefits did not result solely from the sales automation project. There were other factors, including market conditions and growing recognition of HP's product quality. To ensure that the results are not overstated in the ROI analysis, only the improvement in sales productivity will be used. Cost reduction benefits are not included. Further, the benefit of the sales automation program is discounted by using a variable margin of 10 percent.

Analytical assumptions

❏ Revenues will increase from $1.6 to $5 million per sales rep over the period 1993 to 1997.

❏ The company's historical variable contribution margin has been 25 percent. The variable margin for the sales automation project is assumed to be 10 percent.

❏ Operating costs have increased because of the creation of configuration support and sales support teams:

■ Sales support with a loaded labor rate of $90,000 p.a.

■ Configuration support with a loaded labor rate of $120,000 p.a.

❏ Incremental operating costs

■ Computer maintenance

- System training and support
- Software upgrades
- ❏ Capital investment
  - Desktop computer for each sales person @ $6,500/per in 1993
  - Addition of a notebook computer in 1995 @ $5,500/per in 1995
  - Software purchased
  - Straight-line depreciation over four years
- ❏ Tax rate assumed to be 50 percent

Capital investment   Most of the incremental investments are considered to be capital investments. The total expenditures for hardware (including hardware to enable sales reps to work at home) were $9,100,000 in 1993 and $7,700,000 in 1995. Initial software acquisition costs and media conversion costs were $4,900,000 in 1993 and 1995. Money has been included for modifications (recurrency development) to the original programs. The initial capital investments are shown in the cash flow analysis (Table 4–3) as negative cash flows in period zero.

The effect of depreciating capital investment is shown in Table 4–2.

		Depreciated costs in detail			
Capital investments		**1**	**2**	**3**	**4**
Year 1	($14)	$4	$4	$4	$4
Year 2	($5)		$1	$1	$1
Year 3	($13)			$3	$3
Year 4	($5)				$1
Annual depreciation expense		$4	$5	$8	$9

Table 4–2. Depreciation reduces the impact of hardware and software expenditures.

	Year					
	0	**1**	**2**	**3**	**4**	**Total**
Revenue increase		$935	$935	$935	$935	$3,740
Variable contrib.		$94	$94	$94	$94	$374
Increase in operating expenses						
Depreciation		($4)	($5)	($8)	($9)	($26)
Configuration support		($6)	($6)	($7)	($7)	($26)
Field specialists		($11)	($11)	($12)	($13)	($47)
Training and support		($6)	($2)	($6)	($2)	($17)
Net increase in operating expenses		($27)	($25)	($34)	($31)	($116)
Profit before taxes		$66	$69	$60	$63	$258
Taxes		($33)	($34)	($30)	($31)	($129)
Net income after taxes		$33	$34	$30	$31	$129
Adjust for non-cash items						
Add back depreciation		$4	$5	$9	$7	$25
Subtract investments						
Hardware	($11)	($2)	($8)	($2)	($5)	($27)
Software, upgrades	($7)	($1)	($4)	($1)	($4)	($15)
Cash impact on operations	($18)	$35	$28	$36	$30	$113
Cumulative cash flow	($18)	$17	$45	$81	$112	
Discounted cash flow @ 15% discount rate	($18)	$30	$21	$24	$17	
Cumulative net present value	($18)	$13	$34	$58	$75	
Internal rate of return					187%	

Note: Figures are in millions

Table 4–3. Cash flow analysis—return on investment

Determine the costs   Operating costs increased in three areas: configuration support, field specialists, and training.

Configuration support teams were created to ensure that sales reps could get 24-hour turnaround on system configurations. The analysis assumes 50 employees were assigned to the teams with loaded salaries of $120,000 p.a., which increases operating costs by $6,000,000 in 1994.

Operating costs also increased because 120 field specialists were added to support the sales reps. This resulted in an increase of $11,000,000.

Finally, although HP was successful in using lunch and after-work forums for ongoing training, there are ongoing training expenses related to the introduction of new technologies and tools. In 1994 and 1996 the training expenses were assumed to be $4,500 per sales rep for an annual expense of $6,300,000.

Determine the cumulative ROI   Table 4–3 details the annual operating results from the investment in the sales automation solution. The increase in revenue is based solely on increases in productivity, year by year, by all of the sales representatives. It was assumed to be zero in year zero. In year one, the productivity of each sales rep increased from $1.6 to $2.27 million, for a total increase in revenue of $935 million. The incremental contribution for the whole sales force was determined to be $94 million based on the assumed variable contribution margin of 10 percent. After taxes, the increase in income was $33 million in the first year and $129 million over the four-year period.

The cumulative cash flow for the sales automation solution was $112 million, with a net present value of $75 million (discounted at an estimated 15 percent cost of capital). The internal rate of return was 187 percent.

The return on investment based solely on improvements in sales productivity is substantial. The addition of other savings and improvements in customer satisfaction would improve the picture, but they are not needed to justify current and planned expenditures.

Long-term plans   In the near future, HP will provide an interactive media catalog that could provide the basis for presentations and learning modules. A portable configuration and quotation tool set will be provided so sales reps can prepare system configuration and quotes in the field. The system configuration teams will be needed only for complex systems.

Beginning in 1997, the company will be in a position to provide direct access to customers so they can configure, price, and order systems without going through HP employees. Networked interactive media technologies will enable customers to access the information and tools they need.

Although this case study is based on the selling process, it aptly illustrates the effective use of the methodologies and models described in this book. It also serves as a reminder that human resources can be applied to generate highly satisfactory results in the absence of acceptable technological solutions. There is no substitute for competent project management. In the long term, interactive media will enable Hewlett-Packard to achieve breakthrough results.

NOTE

[1] The method has been simplified to make it easy to use by individuals who are not financial experts.

5

Interactive Media in Distribution

The distribution process includes marketing, sales, warehousing and distribution, and customer service—representing a continuum focused on the customer. Marketing, sales, and customer service have recently made extensive use of interactive media. Warehousing and distribution will take advantage of interactive media when electronic commerce matures on the Web. However, the opportunity extends beyond current standalone applications to solutions that provide an infrastructure to support all four. Clearly, there is good justification for combining the processes. All four processes are based on relationships with customers.

- ❏ Marketing is the process of discovering what customers want and need, and directing the efforts of your company to match those needs.
- ❏ Sales is the process of delivering goods and services to the customer.
- ❏ Warehousing/distribution is the process that incorporates order processing, fulfillment, and shipping.
- ❏ Customer service is the process of serving the needs of the customer before, during, and after the sale.

The real opportunity is to direct interactive media at the customer and the customer's buying process. Not only do we want to enhance the process itself, but we must also determine which computer and communications technologies and corporate know-how should be applied to enhance performance as well.

The seller's opportunity to create advantage hinges on the interaction of four processes—customer service, warehousing and distribution, marketing, and sales—with the customer's buying process (see Figure 5–1). All of the events in the buying process impact relationships with customers and provide relevance to activities in the four process areas. Thus, it is critical that networked interactive media be applied to create advantage throughout the buying process. The fact that the greatest payback may result from a solution that combines

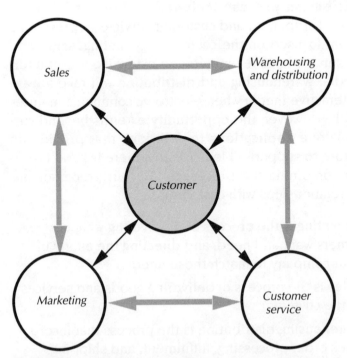

Figure 5–1. Interactions between the customer's buying process and the vendor's distribution processes

all four processes does not mean that they should be combined from the start.

History teaches that it is easier to start with a small, manageable piece likely to demonstrate success and grow into the rest of the opportunity. Notwithstanding this statement, it is critical that all of the target processes are thoroughly understood so that the infrastructure decisions can be based on the whole, rather than on parts of the core process.

If enhancing customer service is a primary corporate goal, start with customer service, but ensure that sales and marketing can be added in the future. If increased revenue is the goal, then we should ensure that the sales automation system will be able to incorporate customer service and marketing at a later time, and so on.

To start, we need to analyze and flow chart each activity, beginning with the customer's buying process. Once we understand the processes, the mission of the company, and the technologies available to enhance the process, we are ready to proceed.

The Buying Process

Customer buying processes vary significantly by industry, by product, by the company itself, by the significance of the procurement, and by a number of other factors. In some cases, the buying process takes place during a single meeting with a sales representative; in others it may take 10 or 20 sessions with a number of different sales representatives. In some cases, such as bidding on government contracts, it is a very formal process with rules that must be obeyed or the selling organization will be disqualified.

Experienced sales representatives know and understand the buying processes of their customers and use this knowledge to their advantage. There is every reason why the selling process should match the buying process as a fundamental tenet of doing business. Yet, that may not be enough. The buying process may be changing and may require changes to the selling process.

It is critical to monitor the buying process in order to understand what is changing and why it is changing. For example, before Abbott Laboratories introduced a new kidney medicine, it surveyed some of the doctors whom the company served. The company determined that doctors' offices were undergoing the same types of changes as other businesses.

Doctors were under pressure to enhance productivity, improve service, and reduce costs. Seemingly, they did not have enough time to investigate all the new drugs that entered the market.

Abbott chose to make it easy for doctors to buy their new kidney drug, Calcijex. The Abbott sales force introduced Calcijex during a brief visit to the doctors' offices, leaving behind a computer diskette that doctors could use to calculate the appropriate dosage based on inputs from the patient's medical records. It also alerted them to potential incompatibilities with other drugs the patient was taking. It then prepared a bill for the treatment. In addition, the diskette contained a complete bibliography of test results. The sales process matched the current buying process and the needs of the buyer perfectly.

The Deere Power Systems Group (DPSG), a division of Deere & Company, determined that it was important to show accurate, custom engine configurations while the sales representative was at the customer's location. In addition to configurations that matched the customer's requirements, the sales representatives needed to provide up-to-date product specifications, quotations, and other information needed by the customer to make a purchase decision. DPSG decided to develop a solution that enabled sales representatives to deliver timely information directly to the customer. The company equipped its sales reps with Macintosh Powerbook computers that included a product configurator, quotation tools, and a product catalog.

As a sales organization, you should model your customers' buying processes using these methods:

1. Surveying sales representatives to establish a base-line understanding of customer buying processes

2. Surveying customers to model their buying processes

3. Determining who influences the selection process

4. Finding out how the influencers relate to individuals and groups in your company

5. Developing an understanding of past and future changes that impact the buying process

6. Reviewing the results with senior members of your sales force

In this discovery process, you may also find that your company is doing things that make it difficult for your customer to buy products and/or services from you. In addition, you may learn what your customers value in their relationship with vendors. You may discover exactly what they need to make a purchase decision in your favor.

The personal anecdote that follows is included to demonstrate how far out of sync companies can get with their customers. It is about a company that had lost its leadership position in the marketplace. It is about a company that was about to lose many of its largest customers to competitors.

Several years ago, I was asked to conduct a customer survey on behalf of one of my clients. Unfortunately, my client had not maintained good relations with its customers—for a variety of reasons. The sales representatives were working hard to make up for the lack of understanding between their management team and their customers. There was no form of contact between the management team and their customers except for an annual users group meeting that was attended by an unhappy group of customers in the previous year.

Products were being designed that failed to match the needs of the vendors' customer base. Sales were declining at a time when other vendors were enjoying significant growth.

The company's customers and the sales reps were glad to see me because I represented a feedback channel directly to the CEO and the vice president of marketing. Almost all of the customers I visited indicated that they would not buy products from my client in the future unless significant changes were made.

I recommended that the CEO buy airplane tickets for every one of the executives and that all of them, including the CEO, visit all their customers to begin rebuilding relationships. In addition, senior management needed to learn first-hand about their selling situation and their customers' buying situations. At best, the company could only hope to keep some of its customers after so many years of neglect.

The Marketing Process

Marketing is the process of uncovering customer needs and wants and directing your company's efforts to satisfying them. It increasingly must take into account the dynamic changes that are taking place in industries and markets. The Internet and, in particular, the Web provide new opportunities to promote products, communicate concepts, and disseminate information regardless of the size and location of an organization.

The pace of change has affected marketing in the same way that it is affecting all parts of the business. It is often difficult to keep up with competitive products and with customer preferences because product development cycles have been shortened dramatically. In addition, there is more competition, and technologies are becoming increasingly sophisticated. In some cases, there are dramatic prospects for growth (for example, almost anything related to the Internet), and in others growth may be slow or declining (for example, newspaper publishing).

While the changes tend to be more volatile in high-technology industries, almost all industries are becoming more dependent on state-of-the-art technology. There is a decided shift away from our industrial base to an information/knowledge base, which dictates the use of computing and communications technologies and digitized content. Companies often focus on primary competitors, sometimes overlooking the real challenges that come from old ways of thinking in marketing.

A marketing process that applies to companies in most industrial sectors is summarized in Table 5–1.

The increased velocity of product introductions is forcing companies to undertake new approaches to marketing. Often it is a reactive approach, because the qualitative and quantitative information needed by marketing groups has not been available in time. In many instances, companies must rely on the experience of seasoned veterans in that industry. However, the Web offers some new ways to interact with customers and prospective customers that can provide a bonanza of qualitative information.

A key ingredient that has been missing in market research is the ability to gather real-time feedback from customers. The feedback and analysis tools developed by DiaCom are designed to improve customer relations and provide feedback using a variety of technologies and, most particularly, the Web.

For example, suppose that a customer who recently purchased an Eagle Talon decides to provide some feedback about some aspect of the design of the seats. The customer would access the Chrysler Technology Center Web page and navigate through the showroom to find the model in question.

If Chrysler were to use DiaCom's products, its customers would be able to select the car's interior on the specifications

Corporate Mission	Market Research	Positioning Strategy
Examine core strengths, expectations, and goals	Conduct qualitative research	Develop a product position
Determine market attitudes, perceptions, and trends	Conduct quantitative research	Develop a market position
Develop a mission consistent with the above	Talk to key members in the target industry	Develop a corporate position

Table 5–1. Marketing process for most industrial sectors

page, select the seat back in the photograph of the Eagle Talon, and then request the feedback mode. After selecting the seat-recliner mechanism from the available options, the customer would be able to indicate that a design change would be highly desirable—for example, allowing the seat to recline all the way.

DiaCom's patented "Distributed Dialogue Processing™" technology makes excellent use of context-sensitive dialogue boxes and an intuitive graphical interface to reduce the amount of text that needs to be entered. The whole operation is "point and click" except for typing in the brief text message. This type of feedback mechanism could significantly improve customer service. And it would make it easier for Chrysler to respond. The company could, at a minimum, send an e-mail message and then act on the feedback—if the suggestion truly represented a defect or improvement suggestion that warranted redesign.

Feedback at this level could be a bonanza for Chrysler or any other manufacturer or service provider. The Web would enable vendors to capture and analyze feedback and respond to their customers. A whole new level of customer service could be provided that would surpass anything that is available now.

In the current consumer environment, most of us would not be willing to take the trouble to phone someone or write a letter. Our expectation is that it is too difficult to find the right person in a large organization and that our feedback would be ignored.

DiaCom also provides a feedback analysis tool that allows marketing or customer service to "fly through," to analyze, and to understand the feedback. For the example cited above, it would group and analyze all of the feedback about seats in the Eagle Talon.

Timely feedback is the key to success. It is the missing ingredient in current marketing and customer service processes. The DiaCom solution allows the seller to capture customer feedback in real time at the moment of need. Important feedback from the buyer should be used to refine the product and/or service offering. This ensures that it truly matches the buyer's needs and wants.

The Selling Process

To be successful, the selling process depends on the efforts of many individuals and groups in the corporation. It is often the oldest process in a corporation and generally the least understood. It is a process that has a significant impact on revenue and profitability and on customer satisfaction— which tend to rank high in the objectives of senior managers.

For many companies today, contact with customers takes place from remote office locations. In some cases, companies have abandoned field sales offices in favor of home offices. Thus the sales process depends on individuals located at the edge of the company's network. As a result, it is important to consider how best to communicate with field sales people and how to provide access to the tools and information they need to perform their jobs.

Although the prospect for broadband services to the home office or to field offices is brighter than ever, it will likely be several years before the network is upgraded to support these services. In most instances, lower-speed networks based on modems at 28.8 kbps or ISDN at up to 144 kbps are the most cost-effective solutions. Many companies use CD-ROMs to send bulk information to field representatives on a periodic basis and the Internet or intranets to provide access to more volatile information. This hybrid solution seems to be adequate for the moment.

Each corporation has its own selling process, and many have more than one. However, the starting point for sales performance support solutions is not the selling process, but the buying process of corporate clients.

Table 5–2 portrays a process used to sell business solutions to corporations. As shown, there are four stages in this process with multiple activities in each stage.

Prospecting	Qualifying	Developing	Closing
Cold calls	Send literature	Create proposal and/or presentation	Fine-tune proposal
Direct mail	Qualify by phone	Visit client to demo/propose	Quote delivery and availability
Seminars	Make appointments	Respond to questions and objections	Sign contract
Referrals	Send demo or sample	Get pricing approval	Collect money
Advertising	Follow-up activities	Follow-up activities	Follow-up activities

Table 5–2. Four stages of a typical business-to-business sales process and activities

In the prospecting stage, the objective is to identify relatively large numbers of potential opportunities. The only thing known for certain is that the prospect has a need that the sales representative believes the corporation can satisfy. Follow-up activities will determine which of the prospects move to the qualifying stage.

In the second stage, using various filters or qualifying parameters, these numbers are reduced to a group that is likely to buy the products and/or services being offered. Usually the prospective buyer indicates that he or she intends to proceed with the project. The seller determines that his or her company is competitive for this opportunity. In addition, the sales representative knows that the potential buyer believes that his or her company is a qualified vendor.

In the third stage, all major objections are satisfied. The sales person has determined that his company will be a finalist and attempts to position his or her company as the vendor of choice. Often this effort is accomplished by developing a champion in the account.[1]

In the final stage, most or all of the competition is eliminated and the probability of getting the order is quite high.

Funds for the project are available and allocated by the buyer. Negotiations are underway.

Your overall understanding of a business process is enhanced when the perspectives of all the stakeholders are well understood. In sales it is important to look at the current buying process of potential customers to ensure that there is a good match between the buying and selling processes.

A good match means that the seller's activities dovetail with the expectations and practices of the buyer:

- ❑ *Timeliness*—bids must be delivered on time, quotations should be provided within a reasonable timeframe, and responses to questions or objections should occur as rapidly as demanded by the situation.
  Deere Power Systems Group and McDonnell Douglas Helicopter used technology to ensure that their sales reps could configure products and provide quotations while at the customers' sites.

- ❑ *Completeness*—provide all of the information needed for the buyer to make a decision in your favor.
  Sales reps for Abbott Laboratories delivered all of the information and tools that medical doctors needed to buy and use Calcijex.

- ❑ *Appropriateness*—conduct sales campaigns that match the rituals of the buying process.

When I was selling computers to the Canadian government in the early 1970s, our branch sales office learned everything it could about the procurement process. In some bid situations we were able to leverage our knowledge of the rules to eliminate some of our competitors or to negotiate a more favorable contract.

By working backward through the sales process, you can pinpoint all of the groups in the company that influence the customer. From that perspective you can determine all of the areas where the sales representative and others can make the prospect's buying decision easier—and in your favor.

The selling process must work with all other groups in the company that interface to the customer; for example, accounting, customer service, maintenance and installation, manufacturing, marketing, product management, shipping, systems analysts, and training. In a number of instances, the other internal organizations are the holders of information that the sales representative needs in order to be effective in the field.

Ideally, the activities of all groups should be coordinated to ensure that the sales process will be most effective. The sales representative must have up-to-date pricing, availability, and delivery information. Customer service and sales representatives need to be aware of problems that the customer is experiencing. And manufacturing needs all of the "build-to-order" information for each customer.

By looking at the process from the perspective of all the stakeholders, it is evident that selling really is a process and not a discrete event. When an order is received or an account is lost to the competition, it is because the process succeeded or failed. Success or failure can seldom be attributed to a single event. Studies of the best sales forces in the United States reveal that a structured sales process, as described above, is one of the keys to success.

The Customer Sevice Process

Customer service is gaining new prominence since it may provide the most important, if not the only sustainable, marketing edge in the digital economy. In an era of short product cycles and rapid technological evolution/obsolescence, it is increasingly difficult for companies to maintain an edge based solely on product design. Many computer companies, for example, have abandoned proprietary hardware technology in favor of industry-standard platforms. The playing field has leveled so that companies must look for new ways to create distinctive value.

Customers have more choice than ever before and are demanding better service. If better service is not forthcoming, customers will readily switch to firms that are able and willing to provide it. One of the key questions that should be asked is: "Is customer service an obligation or an opportunity?"

If it is viewed as an obligation, customer service is an expense that companies want to minimize. Little attention will be given to taking advantage of contact with customers to sell more products and services. As a cost-driven exercise, customer service is not measured by customer satisfaction or contribution to sales. Those of us who have waited at length on the telephone for a response from computer hardware or software suppliers don't believe that we receive good customer service.

If customer service is recognized as an opportunity to distinguish your company, to generate add-on sales, to gather market data, and to increase customer satisfaction, cost is *not* the primary issue. Good customer service becomes the glue that bonds your customers to your company.

High-quality products are the ante in the sales game. Without good products, you're not even *in* the game. But the winning hand should be based on delivery of service excellence. As is manifest by the experience of Federal Express with its Web site, good customer service can be achieved by providing the tools and information customers need to look after themselves.

Customer service excellence is achieved by the following:

❑ Making it totally unacceptable for anyone in the corporation to deliver anything less than superb service

❑ Ensuring that appropriate individuals in the corporation have access to the information and knowledge demanded by the situation

The often-quoted example set by Disney at its theme parks is worthy of mention. Every customer is treated as a guest, and the park is clean because it is simply unacceptable for it to be any other way. Other theme parks find it difficult or impossible to match Disney's example because they have not instilled the same set of values throughout their organizations.

Customer service is simply the process of looking after the immediate and long-term needs and wants of your customers. Often the process is triggered by a customer who wants information or needs help with a problem. The quality of your customer service is dictated by the ability of every person to respond to the customer's request with up-to-date information about the status of information requests, orders, service problems, spare parts, etc.

If a customer's CEO calls your CEO at 7:00 p.m. on a Friday night to discuss a particularly vexing problem, your CEO should be able to retrieve and review the customer's file so that an appropriate response can be made. If your CEO decides that more resources need to be put to the task, the customer file should be updated to reflect this commitment. World-class customer service is the responsibility of everyone who comes in contact with your customers.

Your sales force should not be making calls on existing clients without being aware of current problems and their status. Field technicians should have access to a simple mechanism that allows them to alert the appropriate sales representative to the problem.

In a nutshell, the ideal customer service system should enable:

- Every employee to contribute to sales
- Every salesperson to deliver superb customer service
- Your marketing department to gather timely and accurate data
- Any employee to make fact-based decisions

To satisfy the objectives noted above, the customer service system should ensure that a single file exists for each customer. This file should contain information concerning interactions between the customer and sales, marketing, and customer service personnel, and any others who interact with your customers.

When viewed from the perspective of your customers, it is likely they would value a customer service environment that enabled its employees to do the following:

❑ Provide quick and accurate responses to questions

❑ Be aware of appropriate individuals and groups in your customer's organization

❑ Be aware of customer preferences

❑ Receive and respond to feedback about potential product improvements

❑ Develop marketing efforts in response to the stated needs of your customers

Where and how does networked interactive media fit into the customer service environment? An interactive media product catalog could be invaluable to employees when they describe product attributes and benefits to a customer. The implementation of computer telephony integration (CTI) technology can take advantage of the nationwide Caller ID service from telephone companies to automatically retrieve the appropriate database on receipt of the customer's phone number. (Refer to the "Computer Telephony Integration" sidebar for more information.)

In addition, CTI technology could allow your employees to transfer the voice call and the database information to the most appropriate individuals in your company. Customers would not be forced to repeat the information they have already provided. Each person they talk to can be fully aware of the customer's situation.

Any system with the attributes described above can not only help provide superb customer service, but it can enable your company to keep customers for life. It can also turn customer service into a process that generates new sales leads, provides information about customer needs and wants, and closes more business transactions.

COMPUTER TELEPHONY INTEGRATION

Computer telephony integration (CTI) is not a new idea but one that has taken a number of years to develop into a significant opportunity. Its origins lie in the links that were established between private branch exchanges or PBXs and voice messaging systems in the 1970s. Both hardware and software links were needed between the central processor of the PBX and the computer that managed the messaging system. This "command and status link" enabled the PBX to automatically transfer an incoming call to the voice messaging system if the called party did not answer after several rings. Once a message had been received by the messaging system, it could alert the PBX that a message was available for a specific individual so the PBX could turn on the message waiting light on the individual's telephone set.

To the chagrin of the voice messaging community, the links were all proprietary, so each vendor was obliged to develop solutions for each of the different PBXs—typically those of AT&T, Northern Telecom (now Nortel), and Rolm. Although these command and status links were expensive, voice messaging could be automated, which was attractive to both end users and vendors.

In the early 1980s, Nortel conducted a number of trials that linked computers to PBXs; the results indicated that significant productivity improvements could be made for incoming and outgoing call processing applications. Nortel's vision for computer integrated telephony (CIT) was not realized until 1986 when Digital Equipment Corporation agreed that it had sufficient merit to warrant an investment in 1986. Digital's efforts sparked the interest of the computer community;

COMPUTER TELEPHONY INTEGRATION (continued)

however, progress was marred by the lack of standards.

In the early 1990s, two standards were developed for CTI. The first, TSAPI (Telephony Services Application Programming Interface), is PBX-centric and is based on a standard developed by AT&T and Novell. The second, TAPI (Telephony Application Programming Interface), is personal computer-centric and based on the efforts of Microsoft and Intel.

To implement TSAPI, you establish a link between a PBX and a server. No additional hardware is required at the desktop. Calls placed from a personal computer generate a request that passes through the server, which translates them and passes them on to the PBX. The application software resides in the server.

TAPI uses a telephone link at the desktop rather than a server, and requires additional personal computer hardware. Call requests are interpreted by the personal computer and passed to the PBX using a signaling channel from each telephone set to the PBX. The application software resides in each personal computer.

Similar applications can be generated using either TSAPI or TAPI. For example, in a credit collection application, the server or computer could request that the PBX place calls to debtors based on a database. When the called parties answer, they would be connected to an available operator and the debtors file would be displayed automatically on the operator's screen.

In a customer service environment, CTI technology could allow your employee to transfer the voice call and the database information to the most

COMPUTER TELEPHONY INTEGRATION (*continued*)

appropriate individuals in your company.
Customers would not be forced to repeat the information they have already provided. Each person they talk to can be fully aware of the customer's situation.

The Advertising Process

The advertising process is driven by the need for advertisers to reach their target audiences. Advertising recently split into two distinct processes—traditional mass marketing communications and one-on-one or pointcast communications. The former is epitomized by television, radio, and print advertising and promotion; the latter by the Web or interactive television.

Traditional advertising is a "push" paradigm based on multiple presentations of the advertisement to ensure that the user recognizes the brand. A frequency of three times has become the industry rule of thumb for traditional advertising. Advertising is targeted at and delivered to audiences based on demographic profiles. Popular programs that deliver the largest target audience are able to command the highest rates.

Broadcast television delivers mass audiences so there are always some viewers for which an ad may be inappropriate. The industry spends a good deal of time, effort, and money trying to determine who is really watching television; listening to radio; or reading newspapers, magazines, and other forms of print media. People meters are used in 20 markets (Nielsen) to gather demographic information and (paper) diaries are used in the remaining 190 markets to complete viewer profiles for broadcast television.

Advertisers want to deliver their messages to target audiences. The major networks (ABC, CBS, NBC, and Fox) have been looking at cable networks, interactive television networks, and the Web as vehicles that could allow them to be more effective at reaching target audiences. Ideally, advertisers want to know that their ads are reaching the targeted audience and that viewers are purchasing products and services based on the ads.

Interactive advertising on the Web is a "pull" paradigm which dictates that you provide content of value to viewers or they will not return. The Web offers great potential for growth, but the advertiser still needs to determine how to reach the target audience. Both Web sites and ads must be designed to attract viewers who match the demographic profiles established by advertisers.

In an environment where there are millions of Web sites from which to choose, the problem of matching the buyer and seller is not trivial. The viewer must find the advertiser in this scenario. Currently advertisers are unable to relate "hits" on an advertisement to purchases of the advertised product. Ultimately, technology advances will allow advertisers to determine that individuals from targeted audiences have seen the ads and then have acted on them by buying products and services using the forthcoming electronic commerce capabilities of the Web. Web-based advertising that is linked directly to selling on-line (made possible by secure electronic commerce transactions) will usher in an entirely new era in retailing.

The interactive television networks planned by cable and telephone companies also have the potential to deliver one-on-one marketing communications. Thus advertising will be targeted at and delivered to specific viewers or groups based on demographic profiles. The value proposition of the ad on interactive television will be quite different from that of broadcast television.

Interactive television networks will make it possible to deliver programming at the request of the viewer. Thus the network will allow the service provider to deliver advertising that is targeted to specific viewers or groups based on their demographic profiles. How will the value of the interactive television ad be determined?

Currently the value of an advertising time slot is directly related to the popularity of a program. The network that broadcasts the Superbowl each year can charge huge amounts for advertising time because it guarantees an exceptionally large audience to the advertisers. This model will likely persist for broadcast television.

The value of advertising time for interactive television networks will have no direct link to program popularity but rather to the demographic profile of individual viewers. Young families might receive minivan or diaper ads while older couples would get ads about vacation cruises—while they are watching the same program (albeit at different times). An individual's demographic profile will dictate the types of ads that are presented—not the programming.

Advertisers can be certain that their messages were received by the target audience. Over any period of time, they will know exactly how many times their ads reached members of the target audience. Thus advertising rates could be linked directly to the overall viewing time of the target audience. High-quality programming will continue to attract large audiences, but it only has value to the advertiser when members of the advertiser's target audience view the program.

In summary, mass media advertising is a passive activity while the Web and potentially interactive television engage in proactive promotion. Although the overall value of proactive advertising is a big concern in advertising circles, no one doubts its potential to create a more intimate relationship and to improve targetability. Demographic information will continue to be of great value, no matter how the ads are delivered.

In this section I will discuss the role that interactive media plays in the traditional mass marketing and the pointcast processes.

Advertising is a significant business that will undergo immense change as the Web and interactive television become major forces in our lives. Total advertising and promotion in the United States exceeded $278 billion in 1995, as

($000)				
Year	Promotional Spending	Measured Media Advertising	Nonmeasured Media Advertising	Total
1995	$119,300	$95,800	$63,585	$278,685
1996	$124,000	$102,900	$68,845	$295,745
1997	$128,600	$108,145	$73,255	$310,000
1998	$133,800	$114,235	$78,090	$326,125

Table 5–3. Total advertising and promotion spending in the United States   *Source: Veronis Suhler & Associates, McCann-Erickson, Wilkofsky Gruen Associates*

shown in Table 5–3. It is made up of promotional spending, measured media, and nonmeasured media in rank order.

Promotional spending includes consumer promotion such as point-of-purchase, coupons and premiums, and trade promotion (meetings and conventions, trade shows, and incentives). Measured media advertising is made up of television, radio, daily newspaper, and magazine spending. Nonmeasured media advertising includes direct mail, Yellow Pages advertising, advertising in weekly newspapers, and outdoor advertising. A fifth category of nonmeasured media advertising includes sports and event sponsorships, farm publications, transit poster displays, and other miscellaneous advertising.

In both business and consumer environments, advertising pays for roughly half the cost of delivering information and entertainment. Clearly, advertising is very significant now and will probably remain so. The shift to one-on-one advertising is likely to be profound as it raises questions about what will change and what will stay the same, and how the value of an ad will be determined.

As shown in Table 5–4, the advertising process, from the perspective of the ad agency, has five distinct phases where interactive media capabilities can be exploited. The brand

Stage	Activities
Selling	• Present capabilities and concepts
Account management	• Review past and in-process creative work • Market research on the Web and other sources • Prepare and deliver presentations
Creative	• Develop concepts and strategies • Retrieve past work • Collaborate with others • Prepare the final ad
Production	• Convert the final ad to client's media of choice
Media	• Placement of ads in radio, television, newspapers, magazines, etc., as appropriate

Table 5–4. The use of interactive media in the advertising process

manager at the advertiser and the account manager at the ad agency are key to the relationship between the companies. The brand manager is responsible for delivering sales through the use of ads. The account executive is responsible for the relationship between the advertiser and the agency.

Once the client has selected a direction for advertising a particular product, the creative group prepares a specification for an ad. After approval of the direction or concept, the creative group prepares a mockup of the actual ad (called a comp). Next the ad copy (text or dialogue) is prepared. Finally the comp, art work, and copy are brought together for final approval.

Multimedia-capable computers are used throughout the process, but the final ad output is usually film for paper-based ads, video tape for television, and audio tape for radio—rather than digital files. The film or video tape or audio tape is sent to the magazines, newspapers, television, and radio networks as appropriate.

Let's look at an example to help explain the process. Based on market research, the brand manager and account executive have learned that:

❏ Brand A is targeted toward professional women between the ages of 25 to 49.

❏ The product is sold by mail order.

❏ The best way to reach the target audience is to use a combination of television, radio, direct mail, magazine, and Internet ads.

While the creative group is preparing ads for each media, the message is being fine-tuned, and personnel in the media research and planning groups are trying to find the best vehicles for each media type. In parallel, the brand manager and account executive are trying to ensure that all of the advertising vehicles tie together. For example, the magazine, television, and radio advertisements can all be used to direct the target audience to the advertiser's Web site.

The production process for an ad is a factory-like process that is similar to manufacturing a product. By and large, the production of an ad is a workflow process that is managed by the production team. As noted above, the ultimate output of the process is analog rather than digital, except for ads appearing on the Internet.

The efforts of the media group are directed toward finding the most cost-effective vehicles for delivering the message to the target audience.

Traditional Advertising

The traditional advertising process has been using computer technology and digitized content for some time, but little use is made of networking technology. Ad agencies use brochures, "leave-behind" diskettes, referrals, and mini-proposals to generate new business. Notebook computers are used to prepare and deliver interactive media presentations highlighting capabilities of the agency as well as what it could do for the advertiser.

Multimedia-capable desktop computers are used in the creative process to prepare the artwork and copy that are used in the ad. However, the final product is a linear video clip, a poster, or a paper-based advertisement. All final products must be indexed and stored for future use. Thus the agency and advertiser must store printed materials, audio and video tapes, as well as digitized creative elements.

Networked interactive media make it possible for individuals and groups in advertising agencies and the advertisers' facilities to store, retrieve, and share digitized content. Desktop videoconferencing with screen and file-sharing capabilities can make it easy for the brand manager and the account executive to collaborate, regardless of location.

Advertising in the fast-paced world of high-tech products is triggered by:

1. New product launches
2. Channel distribution
3. Trade shows or other events

Technologies are moving so quickly that product cycles are compressed. As a result, advertising is often reactive rather than proactive. In market-creation environments, it is sometimes necessary to reposition the advertiser because of the actions of competitors or shifts that occur in the marketplace. It is common practice to proceed on a handshake, but the goal of most agencies is to establish a retainer agreement that gives both parties more freedom. In either case, time is of the essence in this environment. Thus it is critical that the information needed by both advertiser and ad agency be readily available—ideally in digital form.

Statistical demand analysis enables mature industries to understand the relationships between advertising and sales as well as between the sales of an item and related processes. For example, tire sales are directly linked to the sale of new automobiles. Companies in mature industries are driven by the need to create high-quality ads that deliver advertising messages adhering closely to well-established marketing messages. Once again, it is critical that the information needs of both advertiser and agency be satisfied effectively.

Media Databases for Advertising

As noted above, all parties in the advertising business need ready access to information they have stored in text files, print media, and audio and video tapes. Archival information is needed during the sales, account management, and creative processes. Like other industries, global competition has made information flow time critical—time is money when responding to market conditions.

Fortunately, media (video, audio, and print) information management and archiving systems are available from companies such as Aim 21 of New York, NY. Recently Aim 21 was acquired by Reuters New Media, a U.S. subsidiary of Reuters Holdings PLC. Reuters New Media develops new applications for Reuters information and transactions services in business and consumer markets.

As part of a new group called Reuters Marketing Information, Aim 21 will create a full-service offering for advertising agencies, advertisers (brand companies), and the media.

All information is stored in digital form including ads in print, radio, and television advertising. Everything associated with a brand can be stored in a single client/server environment with an SQL database engine. No longer is it difficult to find and retrieve completed advertisements or creative content.

The Aim 21/Brand Driver system enables brand managers and/or account managers to review all of the advertising material created for a particular campaign. The system also allows them to review material over a particular period and select individual items for review or repurposing. Selected items are added to a playlist that can be printed or used as a presentation.

Since all of the advertising material is in digital form, it can be shared remotely between offices in an advertising agency or between individuals or groups in ad agencies and their customers. The addition of desktop videoconferencing with collaborative computing capabilities makes it possible to bring resources together, regardless of location.

The Pillsbury Company in Minneapolis has an archive of some 7,000 television commercials which date back to the 1950s. The commercials are often reused in corporate presentations and in new ads. In the past, staff had to search through numerous tapes to find the segment used and make copies, which was a time-consuming process. Now it is simply a cut-and-paste operation to prepare video tape or digital presentations.

These systems enable agencies and clients to work together more closely, to respond more rapidly, to access larger amounts of creative material more rapidly, and to make better strategic decisions.

Interactive Advertising

The Web provides an opportunity to reach 20 million users now and, according to forecasters, more than 100 million by the end of the decade. In addition, the Web provides a unique opportunity to create a new type of relationship with customers. According to Steve Venuti, president and CEO of LVL Interactive of Palo Alto, California, companies with an installed base want to create Web pages that accomplish the following:

- ❏ Stay in contact with customers
- ❏ Cross-sell to existing customers
- ❏ Advertise and promote products and services
- ❏ Complement their business model
- ❏ Provide better customer service

In 1995, many corporations became "web savvy" and developed a good understanding of what other companies are doing and of available technologies for creating and viewing content. Some companies have begun to create the human infrastructure needed to take full advantage of this new advertising paradigm with the creation of on-line marketing management positions.

The key questions that remain for most companies are: "How do you make business sense out of the Web? How does marketing on the Web fit in with your business model and marketing, selling, and customer service processes? What kind of Web site will work best for your company? What does content mean in the context of your business operation?"

The value of pointcast advertising on the Web is dictated not only by available technology but also by the human infrastructure needed to support this new way of doing business. Video ads have little value if a significant number of viewers do not own interactive media personal computers and appropriate applications software. Web surfers who use modems may find that it takes too long to download Web pages filled with high-quality graphics, images, or video clips. Corporations will develop the expertise needed to make decisions based on both the capabilities and limitations of the current Web infrastructure.

Currently, some companies sell their products through distributors and retail outlets. If they begin to sell directly to end users through the Web, they must set up the infrastructure needed to handle transactions and fulfillment, and they must attempt to maintain good relations with the existing distribution channels.

Some companies that have established Web sites have never had a direct channel to market. For example, Avery Dennison does not have a direct sales force—all of its products are sold through distributors. What will it do when potential customers on the Web want to buy direct and buy now! Clearly the company will be forced to re-examine its distribution strategy, and it may choose to change its market channels.

Unlike traditional advertising operations, interactive media are used to deliver the ad to the audience as well as in the selling and creative processes. The Web provides a perfect opportunity to learn how to use its attributes effectively. Poorly designed and implemented Web pages will get a poor response. With the advent of emerging direct-feedback systems, companies will be able to determine quickly why Web pages work or do not work.

The current Web pages of many companies reflect their organizational structures rather than the needs of the audience they are trying to reach. The Web is unique in that potential buyers look for products and services that are of interest to them. It is in the seller's best interest to use every available promotional vehicle to ensure that buyers can find their Web sites. Pointcast marketing must be audience-centric since the audience is highly unlikely to revisit your Web pages and buy your products and services if you do not provide items of interest and value to your visitors.

Companies must look at customer needs, assess the value of the content they intend to provide, and understand what is appropriate. Forcing a customer to wait several minutes while a beautifully designed graphic fills the screen may actually be counter-productive if all the customer wants and needs is factual product descriptions. It is important for your company to make small "learning" investments in the Web rather than trying to do too much too soon. As the Web and your understanding of its potential mature, then it may be appropriate to make significant investments if it fits your business model.

Clearly, the Web has the potential to change the customer/vendor relationship. Experts agree that commodity products will be bought and sold on the Web as will hard-to-find products and services. Before this can happen, the Web must offer a convenient means for the buyer to find qualified sellers.

In the past, location was usually important to success in selling. In the future, location may not mean anything unless shipping costs make a particular venture noncompetitive.

Case Studies

An advertising case study is followed by two sales case studies. The advertising example provides a dramatic indication of the value of having ready access to information. In this case, networked interactive media enabled a major advertiser to better manage its advertising program and, as a result, save millions of dollars.

The sales case studies illustrate two approaches. Although they are different, they deliver a very satisfactory result to all of the stakeholders—customers, sales representatives, and all other groups in the seller's organization.

Neither of the organizations used the specific methodology recommended in this book, but the overall approaches have many similarities and the overall results were more than acceptable. Both parties understood how to map the information and knowledge needs of the sales force to their customers' buying situations.

Acme Case Study

Acme (a pseudonym) is a global consumer-products goods company, over 100 years old, with annual sales exceeding $8 billion. Although the company would not let us use its real name, Acme agreed that we could share a blind case study. The company competes in a marketplace that is jam-packed with new product activity every year. Acme's annual media expenditures exceed $500 million.

Situation

In the early part of this decade, Acme determined that its global business operations faced three significant challenges:

- ❏ Acme competes in more than 50 countries. Product distribution capabilities and media advertising "made the world smaller," which meant that the company needed to be able to respond to competitive threats more quickly.

- ❏ It was becoming increasingly difficult to manage and analyze the company's advertising strategy vis-à-vis that of its competitors. More advertisements were being produced each year, and the ads existed in a variety of formats (audio, video, still images, and text).

- ❏ Acme competes in four business categories and markets more than two dozen brands. It was critical that global identity and positioning were consistent. The company needed to ensure that its marketing strategy was being executed properly. Further, the company wanted to reduce duplication of effort by sharing ads that could be used in more than one market. In addition, commercials that did not support its strategy were to be eliminated.

In 1993, Acme's global marketing director recognized that a quarterly review of all advertising was essential for developing future strategies. The intent was to provide a forum for reviewing the effectiveness of its own advertisements as well as those of its competitors.

Acme needed a technological solution that enabled its employees to gather all of the advertising information needed for each review in a reasonable amount of time for a reasonable cost. The company believed that it was almost impossible to organize and conduct the reviews without taking advantage of computer and communications technologies. Employees would have been forced to physically find and review all of the print, radio, and television ads stored at various locations around the globe. For example, television commercials were available only on video tape stored by Acme's advertising agencies. In addition, audio tapes for radio and print ads for magazines and newspapers were stored by the ad agencies. Brand and category managers would have had to locate and review the ads. Selected ads would then be used to create a presentation for use in the review meetings.

Acme wanted a solution that would allow employees to:

- ❑ Gather all of the advertisements (video, still images, slides, text) in digitized format
- ❑ Analyze the information during market reviews
- ❑ Apply that knowledge to respond appropriately and to be more competitive in the marketplace

Based on the recommendation of its advertising agency, Acme decided to use the Aim 21/Brand Driver product provided by Reuters Marketing Information.

Brand Driver enables the company to conduct global marketing review meetings three to five times each year. The meetings are attended by executives from all over the world, along with their advertising agency representatives.

The purpose of the meetings is to review current activity in a specific category, analyze the ads from each country, and apply the strategy appropriate to the category. Attendees have access to all of the information they need to analyze all of the advertising and marketing initiatives and to assess (1) the production quality of each ad and its ability to deliver the advertising message and (2) the consistency of the ad in adhering to the marketing strategy. In addition, they can view and analyze the television ads aired by competitors in each country, for all categories.

Brand Driver is used to organize and store all of Acme's ads and those of its competitors. It can be customized for each user, so individual columns can be titled to suit the workflow needs of the user.

The following figures show how an advertising agency might sort the information. The agency can search by scrolling through the "client" window and highlight Acme. Similarly, the brand under consideration—America—can be selected and highlighted to reveal the advertisements associated with the Acme account. Finally, the Acme pizza ad can be selected and displayed. As shown in Figure 5–2, the results of the search provide an image of the ad.

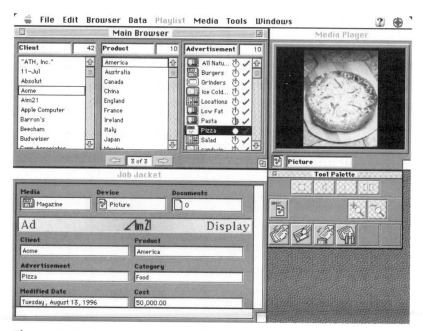

Figure 5–2. Brand Manager allows ad agencies to find and display specific advertisements. *Source: Reuters Marketing Information*

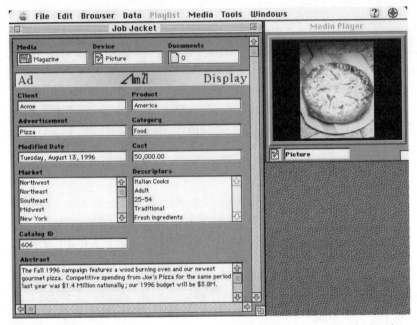

Figure 5–3. The Brand Driver job jacket provides detailed information about the ad and the market.

Source: Reuters Marketing Information

The ad can be enlarged to fill the screen so the viewer can see details as required. In addition, the viewer has access to specific information about the ad in the "Job Jacket" section of the screen (Figure 5–3). The agency can import quarterly sales data, competitive expenditures, and other relevant information. In addition, the Job Jacket offers full Boolean search capabilities so users can find the information they would like to analyze.

By conducting a search for all of the *food* category ads, the agency can create a list of all relevant Acme ads as well as those of its competitors. The user can click on the ads that are of interest and drag them to the Presentation worksheet in the lower right-hand corner (Figure 5–4). The Presentation worksheet can be sent via e-mail to co-workers or to individuals at Acme.

Likewise, an Acme manager can search through the more than 7,000 records stored in the company's database

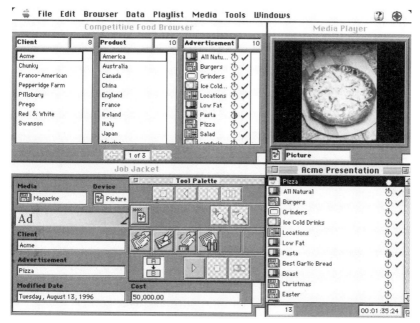

Figure 5–4. All relevant ads can be analyzed for competitive presentations or brand review using Brand Driver.
Source: Reuters Marketing Information

(approximately 6,000 television spots and 1,000 slides), calling up everything associated with a specific category, brand, or competitive entrant. Finally, all of the relevant ads can be used to build a presentation for the review meeting. Brand Driver and media asset management enabled the company to change its advertising and marketing process.

Acme's system is updated on a quarterly basis by Reuters Marketing Information. In the future, the company will extend access to the desktops of all the brand managers at headquarters and at outlying offices. In addition, the company plans to use Brand Manager as a means of improving communication with its advertising agencies. And finally, Acme intends to explore potential applications for its field sales force.

To Acme and its advertising agencies, time equals money. Table 5–5 compares the time it took to prepare for review meetings in 1993 with current practice and projections for

Description	1993	1994	1995	1996	1997 (pro- jected)
Hours per person	200	160	120	80	40
Number of people required	15	12	11	10	4
Total number of hours	3,000	1,920	1,320	800	160
Average cost per meeting[1]	$105,000	$70,560	$50,820	$32,400	$6,800
Total annual cost (four meet- ings per year)	$420,000	$282,240	$203,280	$129,600	$27,200

[1]Annual salaries of employees vary from $25K to $70K—rising from an average $35 per hour in 1993 to $42.50 per hour projected for 1997.

Table 5–5. Acme's cost to prepare global advertising strategy meetings—declining significantly using interactive media software

1996 and 1997. Significant changes include moving from analog to digital media, then upgrading to a network in the future. It is difficult to determine what the costs would have been prior to deployment of the Brand Manager since Acme did not believe that it could be done manually. Television, radio, and print ads are stored by the advertising agencies that serve the company. Acme employees would have needed to get copies of each video tape, search through the tapes to find the appropriate ads, and copy them for later presentation. A similar procedure would have been followed for radio ads. The employees would have been forced to get copies of print ads for use during the meetings. Logistically, it would have been a nightmare!

As shown in Table 5–5, the cost savings are significant, but they pale when compared to savings associated with the improvements Acme has made to its overall advertising campaign. For example, a major objective of the global marketing review meetings is to eliminate ads that do not support specific strategies.

Acme's annual advertising budget is $500 million, so the elimination of one or two ads per year running in multiple markets (countries) can amount to significant savings. Acme noted that it would have been impossible to prepare for and conduct the review meetings without Brand Driver.

The following ROI analysis demonstrates the potential value of a media database for Acme. The calculations are based on the author's experience with payback analysis for similar systems and are representative of the ROI analysis that Acme could have performed.

Analytical Assumptions

Brand driver is used for a growing number of applications in Acme. The analysis which follows is specific to the use of Brand Driver for the global advertising review meetings.

- ❏ The cost of the Brand Driver software is $1,995 per seat.
- ❏ Acme has a service agreement with Reuters Marketing Information that covers client services, service bureau costs, and management of the ad review meetings. Annual expenditures are approximately $810 per seat for more than 10 seats and $900 for less than 10.
- ❏ Macintosh computers with Radius Vision Studio Cards were purchased in 1993 at a cost of $9,500 per seat. In 1997, Power Macintosh computers will be purchased with cards and a network will be installed at a cost of $14,250 per seat.
- ❏ The cost of preparing and conducting each meeting is detailed in Table 5–5. The net decrease in cost from year to year was used in the ROI analysis in Table 5–7.
- ❏ Media cost savings of one-half of 1 percent of the total media budget are realized by reducing the number of off-strategy ads.
- ❏ Existing servers will be used for the next phase of expansion.
- ❏ Straight-line depreciation was used.
- ❏ Corporate tax rate was assumed to be 50 percent.

Business Objectives

The following business objectives can be satisfied by installing Brand Driver at Acme:

- ❑ Increase the number of on-strategy ads to meet marketing objectives
- ❑ Improve quality of advertisements on a global basis
- ❑ Improve the quality and timeliness of presenting Acme and competitive ads
- ❑ Reduce the time needed to prepare for advertising review meetings, which are held three to five times each year

The first step is to determine and quantify the benefits. The second step is to determine the total costs by identifying all of the costs and by depreciating hardware and software costs. The final step is to calculate the cumulative rate of return.

The numbers have been modified to preserve the confidentiality of the company but are indicative of the investment expense and potential cash inflow that can result from effective use of Brand Driver.

Determine Benefits

The first step is to list all the possible benefits under appropriate headings—increased revenues, increased productivity, reduced costs, reduced production costs, improved internal communications, improved client/agency communications—and to quantify the benefits where possible.

- ❑ Increased revenues
- ❑ Reduced costs
- ❑ Improved marketing productivity
- ❑ Improved internal communications

For this analysis, only two quantifiable benefits are being used: reduced costs associated with preparing and conducting the global advertising review meetings and reduced media costs. At each meeting, the company is able to reduce the number of off-strategy ads that would have been aired, which results in significant savings in media costs.

Capital Investment

Most of the incremental expenses of implementing Brand Driver are considered capital investments. The total amount of hardware the first year was $9,500 per seat. The initial software acquisition cost was $1,995 per advertising manager, which represented a total investment of $29,925. The computers will be upgraded in 1997 and installed on a LAN. These initial capital investments are shown in the cash flow analysis (Table 5–7) as negative cash flows in period zero.

Increases in Operating Expenses

Capital assets are depreciated over the life of the program, which in this case is four years. The effect of depreciating the investments is shown in Table 5–6. The numbers in parentheses are the amounts to be depreciated in each year of the program.

Training costs were not incurred since all of the employees were familiar with both the hardware and software.

	Depreciated Costs in Detail ($000)			
Capital Investments	1	2	3	4
Year 1	($172) $43	$43	$43	$43
Year 2				
Year 3				
Year 4	($57)			$14
Annual depreciation expense		$43	$43	$43 $57

Table 5–6. Depreciation reduces the impact of the hardware and software expenditures for Acme.

	($000)* Year				
	1	2	3	4	Total
Decrease in operating expenses					
Reduced media costs (0.5%)	$2,500	$2,625	$2,756	$2,894	$10,775
Meeting preparation costs	$138	$79	$74	$102	$393
Increase in operating expenses					
Depreciation	($43)	($43)	($43)	($57)	($186)
Client service/ maintenance	($10)	($9)	($9)	($4)	($22)
Net decrease in operating expenses	$2,595	$2,661	$2,778	$2,936	$10,970
Adjust for non-cash items					
Add back depreciation	$43	$43	$43	$57	$186
Subtract investments					
Hardware and software				($57)	
Cash impact on operations	$2,638	$2,704	$2,821	$2,936	$10,926
Cumulative cash flow	$2,465	$5,169	$7,990	$10,926	
Discounted cash flow @ 15% discount rate	$2,294	$2,045	$1,855	$1,679	
Cumulative net present value	$2,121	$4,166	$6,021	$7,699	
Internal rate of return				1532%	

* Figures are in thousands

Table 5–7. Cash flow analysis—return on investment for Acme

Cash Flow Analysis—Return on Investment

Table 5–7 details the annual operating results from the investment in Brand Driver. The decrease in meeting preparation costs is based on the amount of savings from year to year with year zero as the baseline. The ROI calculation assumes that there is no incremental contribution because the overall advertising program is more effective. Thus there is no increase in income, and taxes are not included in the calculation.

To convert the income statement to cash flows, non-cash items (normally only depreciation) are added to net income. The internal rate of return is 1532 percent, which is incredible (usually rates of return vary from 50 to 500 percent). In this case, the cost savings realized by reducing the number of off-strategy ads is huge compared to the cost of implementing Aim 21/Brand Driver. As a result, the internal rate of return is correspondingly very large.

The return on investment shown in Table 5–7 is based on savings of one-half of 1 percent. Given that the potential savings could be as high as 5 to 7 percent of the total media advertising budget (starting at $500 million in year one and growing to $579 million in year four), the value of immediate access to all of the advertising of Acme and its competitors is immense.

Apple Computer's ARPLE II Case Study

Apple Computer, a recognized innovator in the information industry and a leader in interactive media technologies, is well known for its easy-to-use personal computers and software. The Macintosh has earned a reputation as an exemplar platform for development and playback of interactive media for multiple platforms.

Based in Cupertino, California, the company offers solutions for business, education, consumer, entertainment, scientific and engineering, and government customers in more than 140 countries. Apple had revenues of $9.8 billion in fiscal year 1996.

Situation

In 1993, Lucy Carter[2] of Apple Computer obtained support to make a significant change in the way that training was delivered to employees. The shift was away from traditional, instructor-led training to performance support systems. Shortly thereafter, the Worldwide Performance Systems organization was established. It became the home of the group that started looking at the information/knowledge needs of Apple's sales channels.

Apple established a task force to examine and create a flow chart of its selling processes. An exhaustive task analysis of the sales process revealed that customized presentations and access to Apple's knowledge base are critical to the success of the sales representatives. Existing training resources, presentation content, and knowledge bases were transformed into the Apple Reference & Performance Learning Experience & Presentation Library (ARPLE).

Originally available only on CD-ROM, ARPLE II is readily available to all Apple employees in the Santa Clara Valley area of California who have access to Apple servers via Ethernet networks. Overall, ARPLE is accessible to more than 20,000 Apple employees, authorized resellers, developers, and value-added resellers (VARs) around the world. Individuals have on-demand access to the companies' sales, marketing, and technical knowledge bases in addition to training materials—no matter how the content is distributed.

Once a month, the CD set is distributed to the Apple field sales force, authorized resellers, developers, and VARs around the world. The set includes a media browser interface, the ARPLE II application which allows users to find, read about, preview, and copy to a hard disk the various media assets available. A wide variety of product and marketing information and data such as presentations, electronic data sheets, QuickTime® movies, and applications software are available to sales personnel. The ARPLE II CD is also available in a client-server version updated on 30 servers each time new editions are released.

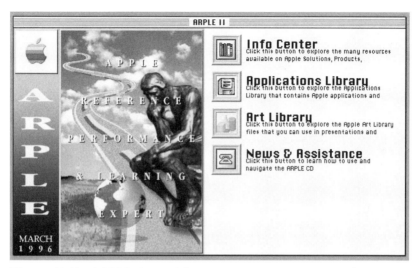

Figure 5–5. ARPLE II provides access to resources, applications and art libraries, and a news and assistance section.

The opening window of the ARPLE II CD-ROM illustrates the major information areas that are available to sales personnel (Figure 5–5).

Users navigate through the CD-ROM to find the information needed for the task at hand. For example, sales reps can review a presentation directed toward meeting the needs of small business establishments, as depicted in Figure 5–6. They can select individual slides to prepare a customized presentation for a prospective client.

Sales reps can review QuickTime movies to ensure that they are up-to-date on the latest information about the PowerPC chips developed jointly by Apple Computer, IBM, and Motorola. By clicking the play button, the movie shown in Figure 5–7 presents the benefits offered by the microprocessor family used in the Power Macintosh product line. As noted, more information is available in the form of an Aldus Persuasion presentation on the ARPLE II CD-ROM.

Almost all of the field personnel in Apple's distribution channels have CD-ROMs. They prefer CD-ROM as a delivery vehicle because it is portable and provides a much faster

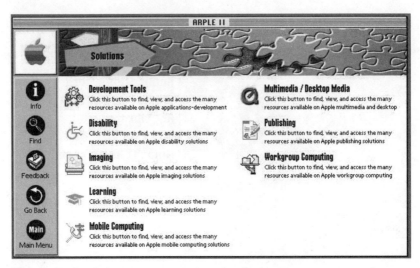

Figure 5–6. Sales representatives have access to presentations and other resources while in the field.

way to access large files than modem access to remote servers. As a rule of thumb, remote access today is acceptable for files that are less than 1 MB. According to surveys conducted by Apple, CDs are preferred for files greater than 1 MB.

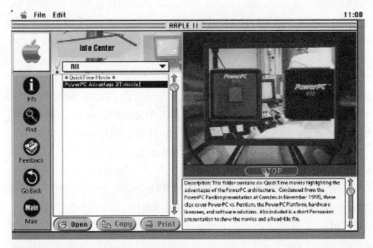

Figure 5–7. ARPLE includes QuickTime movies covering the advantage of the PowerPC.

Apple is investigating the use of the Internet as a means of distributing volatile information. Other companies have found that an intranet capability is a valuable adjunct to information distribution on CDs for time-critical information. Intranets have demonstrated great value. They allow sales representatives to share success stories, learn how to solve problems from their peers, and gather information critical to closing an order.

ARPLE is enhanced continuously based on monthly feedback gathered by Apple's Worldwide Performance Systems organization. It is clear from the abundant feedback that Apple sales representatives rely heavily on ARPLE because it has improved their sales process. Research, competitive information, training materials, and corporate strategies are available when needed during the sales process.

Sales personnel have access to presentation templates, product clip art, and product data sheets so they can quickly prepare customized presentations. Self-paced training courses are provided when ready by other groups in Apple. Contact databases make it easy for field sales to locate support and training personnel.

In the future, Apple's distribution channels could have access to success stories, Apple Solutions, proposal templates, and price lists, all of which could prove to be valuable. Although these items are being considered, none are available at this time.

Internal studies indicate that Apple sales representatives save an average of 11 hours per month because they no longer have to physically search for information. Now it is available through ARPLE. Eleven hours translates into more time in front of potential customers, and as much as three or four more sales calls per month.

The following ROI analysis demonstrates the potential value of a database tailored to the needs of a sales force. The calculations, based on the author's experience with payback analysis for similar systems, are representative of the ROI analysis Apple could have performed.

Analytical Assumptions

❏ The analysis is limited to the revenue and expenses associated with the deployment of ARPLE for the Apple field sales force. Other channels are not included.

❏ The cost of the new hardware needed to deploy ARPLE was $1,000 per sales representative/sales manager.

❏ The cost of the software needed to implement ARPLE was $500 per sales representative/sales manager.

❏ The savings per sales representative that resulted from switching from paper-based to CD-based documentation was $1,000 per sales representative/sales manager per year.

❏ Although ARPLE has the potential to reduce the overall cost of training and preparation of presentations, these savings were not included in the analysis.

❏ Existing servers that housed the databases continued to be used.

❏ The historical variable contribution was assumed to be 33 percent. Variable contribution is a company guideline that is used to determine how much of the increase in revenue should be attributed to the program. It will vary according to the amount of risk that is associated with each program.

❏ Straight-line depreciation was used.

❏ Corporate tax rate was assumed to be 50 percent.

Business Objectives

The following business objectives can be satisfied by the ARPLE program:

❏ Increase sales revenues by improving the productivity of Apple sales representatives

❏ Improve customer relations by providing more timely information

❑ Improve the quality of the selling processes as part of a company-wide total quality system

The first step is to determine and quantify the benefits. The second step is to determine the total costs by identifying all costs and by depreciating hardware and software costs. The final step is to calculate the cumulative rate of return.

The numbers are modified to preserve the confidentiality of Apple Computer but are indicative of the investment expense and potential cash inflow that can result from such an effective performance support system.

Determine Benefits

The first step is to list all of the possible benefits under appropriate headings—increased revenues, increased productivity, reduced costs, improved customer relations—and to quantify the benefits where possible.

❑ Increased revenues

❑ Improved sales productivity

❑ Improved customer service

❑ Reduced documentation costs

❑ Reduced cost of training and presentation preparation

For this analysis, only one quantifiable benefit is being used: increased revenues. Each sales representative's three or four additional sales calls per month should result in increased revenue. Table 5–8 provides a baseline which shows how many sales calls were made per year, how much revenue was generated per year per sales call, and the cost of making a sales call.

The next step is to determine the cash inflow per year that will result from the additional calls. The project team calculated the total number of additional calls per year by multiplying the number of sales reps (1,500) times three additional calls per month times 12 months (54,000 total additional calls per year). They determined the increased net revenue by

No. of sales reps	1,500
Average calls per week per rep	20
	880
Total calls per year	1,320,000
Annual sales revenue	$1,500,000,000
Revenue per sales call	$1,136
Annual sales expenses	$225,000,000
Cost per call	$170
Net revenue per call	$965.91

[1]Based on a 44-work week year

Table 5–8. Determining the net revenue per sales call

multiplying the net revenue per call ($965.91) times the total number of additional calls, and that amounted to $52,159,000. Since the variable contribution for this program is 33 percent, the amount that could be attributed to ARPLE for the ROI analysis was $17,386,000.

Although the system reduces education costs and eliminates the opportunity costs associated with classroom training, the savings are not included in the ROI analysis.

No other benefits were investigated or quantified. The analysis demonstrates that relatively small increases in productivity can lead to three or four more revenue-producing calls per month, per sales rep, which makes it easy to justify a project like ARPLE.

Capital Investment

Most of the incremental expenses of implementing ARPLE are considered to be capital investments. Upgrades to network servers averaged $1,000 per sales representative and sales manager. Thus the total amount of hardware the first year was $1,750,000, with appropriate amounts for upgrades in the following years. The initial software acquisition costs were $500 per sales representative and sales manager. This represented a total of $500,000 in the first year. These initial capital investments are shown in the cash flow analysis (Table 5–10) as negative cash flows in period zero.

Increases in Operating Expenses

Capital assets are depreciated over the life of the program, which in this case is four years. The effect of depreciating the investments is shown in Table 5–9. The numbers in parentheses are the amounts to be depreciated in each year of the program.

In the third and fourth years, assume some hardware maintenance expenses. Training costs were not incurred since all of the sales representatives were familiar with both the hardware and software.

Cash Flow Analysis—Return on Investment

Table 5–10 details the annual operating results from the investment in ARPLE. The increase in revenue is based on the net revenue per sales call (revenue per sales call minus expenses per sales call). The ROI calculation is based on the incremental contribution. As a result of three more calls per month by each sales rep, there is an increase in sales revenue of $17,386,000 in the first year. After taxes, the increase in income in the first year is $9.2 million and over four years is $39.6 million.

To convert the income statement to cash flows, non-cash items (normally only depreciation) are added to net income.

	Depreciated Costs in Detail ($000)			
Capital Investments	**1**	**2**	**3**	**4**
Year 1	($2,625 $656	$656	$656	$656
Year 2	($350)	$88	$88	$88
Year 3	($400)		$100	$100
Year 4	($400)			$100
Annual depreciation expense	$656	$744	$844	$944

Table 5–9. Depreciation reduces the impact of hardware and software expenditures for ARPLE.

	Year ($000)					Total
	0	**1**	**2**	**3**	**4**	**Total**
Revenue increase		$52,159	$54,767	$57,505	$60,381	$224,812
Variable contribution		$17,386	$18,256	$19,168	$20,126	$74,937
Decrease in operating expenses						
Documentation		$1,750	$1,838	$1,929	$2,026	$7,543
Increase in operating expenses						
Depreciation		($656)	($744)	($844)	($944)	($3,188)
Maintenance				($50)	($50)	($100)
Net decrease in operating expenses		$1,094	$1,094	$1,035	$1,122	$4,345
Profit before taxes		$18,480	$19,349	$20,204	$21,249	$79,282
Taxes		($9,240)	($9,675)	($10,102)	($10,624)	($39,641)
Net income after taxes		$9,240	$9,675	$10,102	$10,624	$39,641
Adjust for non-cash items						
Add back depreciation		$875	$964	$1,063	$1,163	$4,064
Subtract investments						
Hardware	($1,750)		($200)	($200)	($200)	($2,350)
Software, upgrades	($875)		($150)	($250)	($200)	($1,425)
Cash impact on operations	($2,625)	$10,115	$10,288	$10,765	$11,387	$39,930
Cumulative cash flow	($2,625)	$7,490	$17,778	$28,543	$39,930	
Discounted cash flow @ 15% discount rate	($2,625)	$8,796	$7,779	$7,078	$6,511	
Cumulative net present value	($2,625)	$6,171	$13,950	$21,028	$27,539	
Internal rate of return					387%	

Table 5–10. Cash flow analysis—return on investment for ARPLE

Capital investments are cash outflows subtracted from the positive cash flows in the appropriate period. The cumulative cash flow for ARPLE was $39.9 million, with a net present value of $27.5 million (discounted at an estimated 15 percent cost of capital). The internal rate of return was 387 percent—a remarkable number! This example is a facsimile prepared by the author and may not be the actual result achieved by Apple Computer, but it indicates the potential of providing performance systems in the field sales environment.

The return on investment is substantial because the investment was relatively small while the increase in sales revenue and the decrease in documentation costs were significant. It also reflects the fact that the type of information provided by ARPLE is a critical success factor in Apple's selling process.

California State Automobile Association

California State Automobile Association (CSAA)[3] provides travel and automobile insurance services to its members. In 1991, CSAA found that it had several challenges and opportunities that needed attention. The company was growing rapidly but it faced both increased competition and increased regulation. CSAA determined that it would be increasingly important to:

❏ Improve member satisfaction with its services

❏ Increase productivity of its employees

❏ Lower overall operating costs

❏ Continue to offer 5Diamond service

The first priority was to improve customer service. The company decided that it needed to train its front-line employees—2,000 employees in 72 locations—so they could play several different roles when dealing with customers. Customers were obliged to deal with a variety of people when they wanted service—a touring counselor, an insurance service representative, a claims assistant, an underwriting service representative, and an adjuster or a claims clerk.

The notion that one person could fill all six roles was highly attractive since CSAA members would always reach the "right" person (Figure 5–8). In order to accomplish this, employees needed to be cross-trained so they could act as member service representatives; they also needed to have access to the information that was pertinent to each of the roles they would be performing.

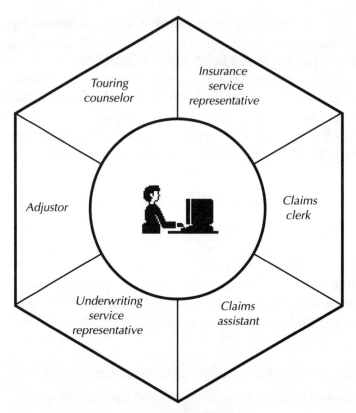

Figure 5–8. Each employee who deals with customers needed to play multiple roles.

CSAA needed to determine how to train 2,000 employees over an 18-month period and how to provide the information they would need on-demand for the various roles they would be asked to perform. The project team quickly determined that a classroom training regime would not allow them to complete the training in time. An Integrated Performance Support System (IPSS) was proposed by Roberta Woolever and the education design team and was implemented by Autumn Wagner and her team.

The IPSS was to include self-paced learning modules, on-line reference materials, job aids, and other information that would be needed by the member service consultant. The business case included the following benefits:

❑ Reduced learning time

❑ Reduced travel and downtime costs

❑ Increased productivity

In addition to the training modules, an interactive help system (On-Line Guide) was developed to provide instant access to information needed to respond to members' requests for information and assistance. The help system contains 10,000 pieces of information and was designed to provide rapid, in-context responses to queries.

Telephone centers were established to off-load the field offices, which were swamped by incoming calls. The employees in the call centers are being trained to act as member service representatives and are supported by the On-Line Guide on a day-to-day basis.

Knowledgebase technology, developed for the On-line Guide by Robertson Associates of Mill Valley, California, displays just-in-time information for CSAA member service representatives. Detailed information can be accessed quickly so that the representatives can respond to members in real time during live phone conversations.

In the example shown in Figure 5–9, the CSAA representative clicked on the Touring area in the main menu, selected Mexico travel to help the member plan a trip, then looked up requirements for using the Mexico Tourist Card.

An independent analysis indicated that that a return on investment of 700 percent could be achieved for the IPSS over a 15-year period.[4]

The IPSS has great potential for other parts of the organization. If underwriting guidelines were available on the IPSS to field offices, premium errors could be reduced because employees would have access to up-to-date information. If CSAA sales representatives were equipped with notebook

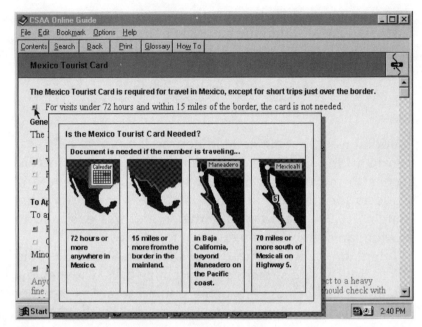

Figure 5–9. Knowledgebase technology makes it easy for service representatives to respond to client inquiries.
Copyright © 1996 California State Automobile Association; Copyright © 1996 Luminaire Multimedia, Inc.; Copyright © 1996 Robertson Associates

computers, they could have instant access to the information in the On-Line Guide related to policies, practices, procedures, and other references.

McDonnell Douglas Helicopter Systems

McDonnell Douglas Corporation is a leading aerospace and defense company that employs nearly 64,000 people worldwide. It designs, develops, manufactures, integrates, and supports military and commercial aircraft, helicopters, missiles, space-launch vehicles and other space systems, and sensing systems.

Helicopter Systems serves U.S. and other national and international armed forces; commercial light-helicopter operators; police forces, and public-service providers, including air ambulance services.

Situation

The headquarters of McDonnell Douglas Helicopter Systems is located in Phoenix, Arizona. A small group of sales personnel and support staff sell helicopters to police forces, military organizations, and corporations around the world.

Helicopters are big-ticket items with an average selling price of $700,000. The configuration is complicated by the fact that there are 540 options. With so many options available, all sales involve customized systems. Most of the sales representatives are pilots well equipped to describe the merits of McDonnell Douglas products.

Prior to 1992, the proposal preparation process took 45 days. The sales representatives met with prospective clients to determine their unique requirements. The requirements were passed on to the engineering group that was responsible for configuring the helicopter to satisfy the customer's needs. Once engineering designed a suitable solution, they drafted a contract and the whole package went to another group for pricing. This 45-day process was far too long in a highly competitive market.

Alan Neugebauer, marketing manager for the MD 500 series helicopters, determined that Macintosh PowerBooks could be used to reduce the sales cycle. This could happen only if software could be acquired or developed reducing the proposal preparation process.

Each PowerBook is loaded with an account information database, an interactive media product catalog, technical descriptions of key components, and maps of worldwide supply depots. Contract terms are stored in a 4th Dimension database. Pricing information, updated daily, is included as well. Engineering rules tables help configure the system while the sales representative is talking to the customer.

For example, the engineering rules operate at two levels. Suppose that a customer wants to replace a searchlight with a camera. The system indicates that there is a conflict and makes a recommendation. There are two final checks—the first is country certification, because each country has its own set of rules and regulations—and the second indicates that the custom configuration will work with the specified extra equipment.

The sales automation system allows the sales representative to accomplish the following:

- ❏ Review the configuration with the customer and get approval
- ❏ Provide financial and competitive analysis information
- ❏ Prepare a formal quotation with approved pricing

The impact on the sales cycle and the ability of the sales representative to close an order has been dramatic. Productivity per sales representative rose from $1,500,000 in 1992 to $4,700,000 in 1995. CIO magazine gave an award to McDonnell Douglas Helicopter Systems in recognition of a sales automation system that resulted in a cumulative ROI of 238 percent in 30 months.

The following ROI analysis is a facsimile of the internal ROI prepared to justify the project. Like most other companies in highly competitive markets, McDonnell Douglas is reluctant to reveal the details. This study clearly demonstrates the potential value of an interactive media database tailored to the needs of a sales force. I based these calculations on my experience with payback analysis for similar systems which I believe are representative of the ROI analysis that McDonnell Douglas could have performed.

Analytical Assumptions

- ❏ McDonnell Douglas Helicopter Systems revenues were $50 million in 1994.
- ❏ The number of sales personnel did not change over the analysis period.
- ❏ The sales support provided by the engineering, contracts and pricing groups was reduced by 15 person days per sale.
- ❏ Fifty percent of the productivity improvement per sales representative is attributed to the sales automation system.

❏ Maintenance and update of the engineering rules, contract clauses, and pricing database added 15 person-days per month in support of the sales process.

❏ Straight-line depreciation was used.

❏ Corporate tax rate was assumed to be 50 percent.

Business Objectives

The following business objectives can be satisfied by the recommended sales automation solution:

❏ Increase sales revenues by improving the productivity of sales representatives

❏ Gain competitive advantage by reducing the sales cycle

❏ Improve customer relations by increasing the credibility of the sales representatives

The first step is to determine and quantify the benefits. The second step is to determine the total costs by identifying all of the costs and by depreciating hardware and software costs. The final step is to calculate the cumulative rate of return.

The numbers have been modified to preserve the confidentiality of the company but are indicative of the investment expense and potential cash inflow that can result from an effective performance support system.

Determine Benefits

The first step is to list all of the possible benefits under appropriate headings—increased revenues, increased productivity, reduced costs, improved customer relations—and to quantify the benefits where possible.

❏ Increased revenues

❏ Improved sales productivity

❏ Reduced sales cycle

❏ Increased credibility of the sales representative

❏ Reduced documentation costs

For this analysis, the quantifiable benefits include increased revenues and reduced sales expenses. Revenue was expected to increase because proposal turnaround time was reduced from 45 days to a single day. This enabled the sales force to make more productive calls per year. The productivity per sales representative increased from $1.5 to $4.7 million over the period from 1992 to 1995. The revenues per year attributed to the sales automation system are 50 percent of the actual increase as shown in Table 5–11. The total variable contribution was $7,140,000 in year two of the project.

Capital Investment

The incremental expenses of implementing sales automation at McDonnell Douglas Helicopter Systems included PowerBook computers for the sales force. The software solution, created for approximately $200,000 (including staff salaries), is based on standard Macintosh products such as MacDraw Pro, the 4th Dimension database, and HyperCard. These initial capital investments are shown in the cash flow analysis (Table 5–13) as negative cash flows in period zero.

Decrease in Operating Expenses

Prior to implementing the system, individuals from the engineering, contracts, and pricing groups provided sales support for every proposal prepared for a potential customer. This was significantly reduced once the engineering rules, contractual terms and conditions, and pricing information

Year	Productivity Improvement	Amount Attributed to Sales Automation	Total Variable Contribution
1992	$0	$0	$0
1993	$1,020,000	$510,000	$7,140,000
1994	$1,050,000	$525,000	$7,350,000
1995	$1,130,000	$565,000	$7,640,000

Table 5–11. Determining the net revenue per sales call for McDonnell Douglas Helicopter Systems

Capital Investments	Depreciated Costs in Detail ($000)			
	1	2	3	4
Year 1	($270)	$67.50	$67.50	$67.50	$67.50
Year 2	($25)		$6.25	$6.25	$6.25
Year 3	($25)			$6.25	$6.25
Year 4	($25)				$6.25
Annual Depreciation Expense		$67.50	$73.75	$80.00	$86.25

Table 5–12. Depreciation reduces the impact of hardware and software expenditures for McDonnell Douglas Helicopter Systems.

were made available to the sales representatives on their notebook computers. The savings amounted to $195,750 in the first year. The savings grew to $654,750 as the orders tripled over the life of the project.

Increases in Operating Expenses

Capital assets were depreciated over a four-year period. The effect of depreciating the investments is shown in Table 5–12. The numbers in parentheses are the amounts to be depreciated in each year of the program.

The company incurred an increase in operating expenses because of the need to update the engineering, contractual, and pricing databases on an ongoing basis. Accordingly, sales incurred some expenses for the time spent by the respective groups maintaining the databases. In the second, third, and fourth years, it was assumed that there would be some hardware maintenance expenses. Training and support costs were $75,000 in the first year with an appropriate amount in subsequent years.

Cash Flow Analysis—Return on Investment

Table 5–13 ROI details the annual operating results from the investment in the sales automation solution. The increase in revenue is based solely on increases in productivity (year-by-year) by all of the sales representatives. In year one, it

	Year ($000)					
	0	**1**	**2**	**3**	**4**	**Total**
Revenue increase		$0	$14,280	$14,700	$15,280	$44,260
Variable contribution		$0	$7,140	$7,350	$7,640	$22,130
Decrease in operating expenses						
Sales support		$195.7	$237.5	$493.5	$654.7	$1,681.5
Increase in operating expenses						
Depreciation		($67.5)	($73.7)	($80)	($86.2)	($307.5)
Database maintenance		($13)	($13.5)	($14.1)	($14.5)	($55.2)
Hardware maintenance		$0	($3.5)	($3.5)	($3.5)	($10.5)
Training and support		($75)	($7.5)	($7.5)	($7.5)	($97.5)
Net decrease in operating expenses		$40.2	$97.5	$232.4	$381.7	$751.8
Profit before taxes		$40.2	$7,238	$7,582	$8,022	$22,882
Taxes		($20.1)	($3,619)	($3,791)	($4,011)	($11,441)
Net income after taxes		$20.1	$3,619	$3,791	$4,011	$11,411
Adjust for non-cash items						
Add back depreciation		$67.5	$73.7	$80	$86.2	$307.5
Subtract investments						
Hardware	($70)		($5)	($5)	($5)	($85)
Software, upgrades	($200)		($20)	($20)	($20)	($260)
Cash impact on operations	($270)	$87.6	$3,668	$3,846	$4,072	$11,403
Cumulative cash flow	($270)	($182.4)	$3,485	$7,331	$11,403	$21,767
Discounted cash flow @ 15% discount rate	($270)	$70.6	$2,773	$2,529	$2,328	$7,431
Cumulative net present value	($270)	($199.4)	$2,574	$5,103	$7,431	
Internal rate of return					337%	

Table 5–13. Cash flow analysis—return on investment for McDonnell Douglas Helicopter Systems

was assumed to be zero; in year two, the productivity of each sales rep increased from $1.5 to $2.52 million, for an increase of $1.02 million. The incremental contribution for the whole sales force was determined to be $7,140,000. After taxes, the increase in income was $20,100 in the first year and $11.4 million over the four-year period.

The cumulative cash flow for the sales automation solution was $22 million, with a net present value of $7.7 million (discounted at an estimated 15 percent cost of capital). The internal rate of return was 337 percent.

The McDonnell-Douglas success story vividly demonstrates the leverage that an organization can obtain using interactive media to deliver the information needed by sales representatives at the right time and place in an appropriate form. Mr. Neugebauer simply applied appropriate technologies to the sales process and "delivered the goods."

NOTES

[1] A champion is an influential individual who agrees to promote the vendor's solution.

[2] Lucy Carter, previously with Apple Computer, is now with Eagle River Interactive in Palo Alto, California

[3] The screen shot relating to the Mexico tourist card and all materials relating to CSAA are used by permission with all rights reserved.

[4] The financial group decided that the project warranted a 15-year return projection because it represented a 15-year cost to CSAA. This is an unusually long term for an ROI analysis.

[4] The financial group decided that the project warranted a 15-year return projection because it represented a 15-year cost to CSAA. This is an unusually long term for an ROI analysis.

6

Interactive Media in Manufacturing

For a number of years, manufacturing operations have included the use of computer and networking technologies in a number of different capacities. The value of computer-integrated manufacturing (CIM), computer-aided design (CAD), and computer-aided manufacturing (CAM) is often discussed in the literature about manufacturing (Kalpakjian, 1992).

Computer-integrated manufacturing is a broad term describing computer integration of all aspects of design, planning, manufacturing, distribution, and management. The technology for implementing CIM is well established; however, it involves the total operation of the company, so it must be comprehensive and have an extensive database that includes, at a minimum, the following items:

- ❏ Product information, such as part shape, dimensions, and specifications
- ❏ Production data, such as the manufacturing processes involved in making the parts or products
- ❏ Operational data, such as scheduling, lot sizes, and assembly requirements
- ❏ Resources data, such as capital, machines, equipment, tooling, and personnel and their capabilities

Computer-aided design involves the use of computers to create design drawings for products. Computer-aided design, or CAD systems, is used in mechanical design and geometric modeling of products and components. CAD systems are used extensively in the design of integrated circuits, circuit boards, and other electronic devices.

Computer-aided manufacturing is defined as the use of computer technology in all phases of manufacturing products—process and production planning, machining, scheduling, management, and quality control. Computer-aided design and computer-aided manufacturing are sometimes combined into CAD/CAM, which enable the transfer of information from design into planning for manufacture without the need to manually reenter part geometry information.

Interactive media can be incorporated throughout the manufacturing process, especially in process stages that involve complex procedures. The need to increase velocity to market has prompted many companies to consider collaborative and computing technologies along with interactive media to allow design experts to participate in product development, regardless of their location.

Information systems planners envision interactive media applications as a means of improving collaboration between geographically dispersed employees and for soliciting feedback from customers, thereby reducing product development time and ensuring customer satisfaction.

For example, a development engineer could show work in progress on-screen to a remote client in the form of a 3-D CAD file in order to get comments and suggestions in real time. The ability to engage customers throughout the development process could significantly reduce the need for time-consuming and expensive redesigns. In addition, by participating in the design of the product, customers can "buy in" at a very early stage and are more likely to remain loyal to their supplier.

Furthermore, collaborative capabilities allow team members to work in parallel rather than in serial fashion. The case studies in this chapter demonstrate how networked interactive media enable team members associated with design, development, and production to operate in a media-rich environment that reduces cycle time and manufacturing costs, increases product quality, and allows the organization to respond more rapidly to change.

For the purpose of this book, the manufacturing process comprises several business processes, including the following:

❑ New product introduction

❑ Production

In this chapter, we will examine a significant shift in the product design process based on the success story at The Boeing Company. When contrasted with the paper nightmare of a traditional product process, utilizing computer and communications technologies with digital content provides a superior performance solution.

Notable improvements have been made to the production process by AlliedSignal Aerospace through the use of electronic assembly instructions based on:

❑ Intelligent interactive media documents with embedded, object-oriented programming. In effect, this is what Sun Microsystems is attempting to do with JAVA applets on the Web.

❑ Unique software configurations that automatically update the embedded software with new revisions, transparent to the user.

❑ Hot text that can load text, graphics, and movies from any system on the network at the click of a button. Again, this is similar to hyperlinked text on the Web.

❑ Multiple media such as 3D objects, images, and movies that can be embedded in manufacturing documents.

All of the above capabilities have become noteworthy because of the incredible amount of attention given to the Internet and the Web. However, they have existed In networked Macintosh environments using production software from Microelectronics, Inc., of Las Vegas, Nevada, for five years. AlliedSignal Aerospace began working with the software in 1992.

In addition, we will look at another form of production related to the development and delivery of "knowledge" products by Booz•Allen & Hamilton to its clients. Both the Boeing and the Booz•Allen & Hamilton success stories are based on multidisciplinary teams that have access to digital content using existing computer and communications technologies. The "factory" outputs are very different—a 550,000-pound aircraft and a paper report—but both demonstrate the advantage gained through the appropriate application of interactive media technologies in business processes. Both recognize the value of intellectual capital in delivering high-quality products and services.

Finally, throughout this chapter there are a number of parallels between the just-in-time concept demonstrated by Toyota Motor Company in 1952 and the capability of performance support systems. Toyota's *kanban*, which means visible record, ensured that the correct parts were delivered where they were needed, when they were needed, on a consistent basis. Kanban resulted in reductions in product cost; inventory; rejection rates; lead times; scrap, rework, and warranty costs; and increases in direct and indirect labor productivity.

When the kanban concept is combined with just-in-time delivery of information and corporate know-how in an interactive media environment, production facilities realize even greater benefits.

Manufacturing

Increasingly, factories are information-intensive environments. Computers are used not only for precision control of production processes but also to deliver just-in-time information and knowledge to workers on the factory floor. Manufacturers are investing in performance solutions based on interactive media capabilities and desktop videoconferencing with collaborative computing capabilities. The shift to just-in-time delivery of knowledge can have a similar and potentially greater impact than the just-in-time delivery processes of parts and materials that Japanese companies introduced in factories.

Performance support solutions that include desktop videoconferencing can improve the transfer of knowledge across relevant departments. Workers on the factory floor can access learning modules that introduce a new assembly procedure or that show how to make a machine adjustment. Color images, animation, and video clips accompany text and graphics to help employees understand the information that is being presented.

At General Machinery, a division of Wheaton Industries, the transition to a paperless manufacturing system, combined with a performance support solution, enabled the company to reduce product development cycle time from 24 months to 10 months. The information is given to factory floor workers at exactly the right moment. Photographs and video clips are synchronized with the text of step-by-step instructions.

Previously, paper-based instructions were sometimes inconsistent because multiple copies of the instructions would become marked up in different ways by different individuals—whereas on-line instructions are collectively annotated and updated as part of the continuing work in progress. With the paperless system, all workers get the same instructions. The computer-based manufacturing system also ensures that the person on the floor gets access to the right expert. As a result, workers on the plant floor do not chase the wrong person.

New Product Introduction Process

The new product introduction process has been a paper-bound and meeting-intensive process. As stated, the goal of the process is to ensure that all of the deliverables of the commercial product specification are complete. A review follows each stage of the process. A variety of personnel, who may be located at a number of different locations, attend these reviews. It is largely a serial process with "go/no go" meetings interspersed at critical points. The process functioned well in the past when product cycles were measured in years, but today, when product development cycles are measured in months, desktop videoconferencing with collaborative computing may be the only way to stay competitive.

Computer and communications technologies were not central to the process, although they were used for some of the tasks. Content was paper-based—not digital. Massive amounts of documentation were prepared for all of the individuals and groups involved in the process. Collaboration occurred at face-to-face meetings and not on an "as-and-when-needed" basis.

Customer input was gathered by sales, marketing, and product management before the process started. Customers had no further involvement until they were asked to beta test or field trial the product. There was little or no direct contact between the design team and customers at any point in the process.

The following example depicts a traditional product development process for a complex computer or communications product. Product development will vary by industry, by company, and even by product line. Thus, readers must ensure that they understand their own product development process thoroughly prior to planning the implementation of individual applications or performance support systems.

Product Development Process

New product introduction is a process that flows from product or service introduction through to implementation and support. Although the process involves continuous review and revision, it maintains the original intent throughout the product development activities. Success is based on meeting the original or revised commercial product specification. Supporting plans and related activities may change as conditions dictate, but the intent of the commercial product specification must be met. The four basic stages of the product introduction process are shown in Table 6–1.

Basic Stages			
Initiation and Definition	**Design and Development**	**Testing and Review**	**Implementation and Support**
Commercial spec	Design reviews	Internal tests	Sales and marketing plans
Specification review	Product management plan	Field trials or beta tests	Marketing communications
Beta Tests			Customer service
R&D approval		Controlled market introduction	Education and testing
			Administration
			Forecast procedures
			Pricing procedures

Table 6–1. Four basic stages of a new product introduction process for telecommunications or computer equipment

Initiation and definition   This set of activities revolves around the commercial product or service specification. The document created at this stage directs investment funds and resources, management attention, and all of the activities that follow. The document draws on market directions and company strategies to drive product development. When the document is complete and approved, it is the basis upon which R&D funding is allocated.

Design and development   The next step is to synthesize the product definition and initial design into a salable product that can be successfully manufactured by the corporation. Design review meetings are used to examine progress, provide new inputs, and determine next steps. During this stage, it is important that product management starts making product introduction plans and begins to enlist the support of sales, service, customer support, training, and other groups throughout the enterprise.

Testing and review   Once the design and development of the product are complete, a technology trial or alpha test is used to determine if the product conforms to the commercial product specification. Technology trial results are used to refine the product as necessary. Upon successful completion of the trial, the product is ready for limited manufacture and field trials or beta tests at selected customer sites.

Implementation and support   Planning for the successful product introduction and launch begins when the new product concept is developed at the outset in the commercial product specification. When the R&D funding is approved, the product management group prepares a product introduction plan. Many different groups in the corporation must support the introduction, including those involved in: pricing, training, sales support, customer service, maintenance, marketing, and manufacturing. The roles of all these groups must be included in the product introduction plan, and they must commit resources to support the product.

Summary   The product introduction process is an integrated series of activities and plans with schedules and checklists to ensure that all of the deliverables of the commercial product specification are completed. The process demands access to corporate knowledge bases and to newly gathered market information. The knowledge needs to be shared among many different individuals and groups who may be in different locations. New product introduction is a good candidate for networked interactive media, since the success of this process ultimately determines the overall success of the corporation.

A thorough understanding of each of the process steps and the role and location of each of the groups makes it possible to determine ways to improve the process utilizing networked interactive media solutions and collaborative computing. For example, it may be possible to shorten the time to market, which could be important to the success of the new product.

In addition, detailed flow charts can be used to establish the metrics needed to calculate the time, money, and

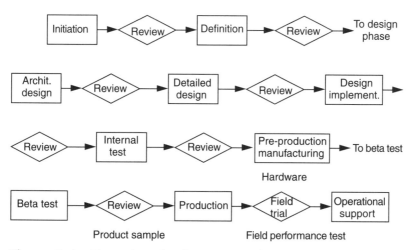

Figure 6–1. Flow chart for the new product introduction process for a hardware product

resources needed to complete each step. This information provides a baseline for making decisions about potential improvements. Figure 6–1 shows a typical flow chart of the new product introduction process for a hardware product.

Of necessity, success in new product development relies on many groups in an organization and many elements of a corporate knowledge base. It appears that there is significant potential for improving the process using networked interactive media solutions.

Collaborative Design

Many companies accept the fact that product life cycles will continue to diminish as global competition increases. When combined with increasing product complexity, these factors have forced many large manufacturing companies to consider the possibilities offered by "concurrent engineering" technologies. Concurrent engineering offers the promise of increased velocity to market because it allows design teams to work in parallel rather than serial mode in the product development process.

The Space Systems Division of Rockwell International is taking advantage of collaborative engineering technologies for the space shuttle program. Real-time collaboration and decision making have been received enthusiastically by engineering staffs located at the Downey and Seal Beach, CA, campuses. Design review meetings and ad-hoc brainstorming discussions are being conducted between sites on an ongoing basis using TeamConference, which was developed by Spectragraphics.

TeamConference is a real-time information-sharing tool for application and whiteboard conferencing between users in remote locations. Participants of a review meeting can be seated at any X-window-enabled workstation, terminal, or PC that is connected to a TCP/IP network and that shares graphics or non-graphics data from such applications as CAD/CAM/CAE.

Product design and development teams often consist of individuals from different groups in different locations around the world. In addition, the use of contract engineering services often means that in-house design teams no longer embody the overall expertise needed to complete the design effort. The problems are exacerbated as more and more of the design effort is outsourced to specialized engineering service companies. Communication and collaboration among these separated groups, both inside and outside the company, become more difficult and could impact the "window of opportunity" for new product introductions.

As we move further into the digital age, success in the increasingly competitive marketplace will be determined by how successfully critical design information can be shared and revised. Expertise must be brought to bear regardless of location. Further, it should be easy to involve customers in the design process. Networked interactive media can provide the media-rich environment needed for success.

The term "collaborative design" describes the nature of the process needed to move forward. Product design decisions can no longer wait until the team can be assembled at the same time and same place; they need to be made in real time. Team members need to be able to collaborate and share critical information when and where it is needed. Design engineers must be able to share 3-D drawings with team members in maintenance, management, manufacturing, product management, and other groups in order to reach critical decisions. In some instances, customer input may be mandatory.

In many market environments, it is no longer feasible for design engineers to plot the design, jump on a plane, and attend various review meetings with each of the needed representatives; accumulate their responses; make the appropriate changes; and send signed-off copies for the final changes via overnight courier. This method of collaboration and information sharing is too time consuming and does not take advantage of media-rich communication.

Large companies such as Boeing, Ford Motor Company, Montsanto, Nortel, and Texas Instruments have invested in collaborative design technologies.

The Boeing Company

On October 15, 1990, Boeing, in conjunction with United Airlines, announced a new airliner that was to be larger than a 767 but smaller than the 747-400. The new aircraft was designated the Boeing 777. Less than four years later, the first production aircraft made its first flight. United Airlines inaugurated Boeing 777 services on June 7, 1995.

The four-year design process cost $4 billion and resulted in a twin-engine aircraft that is 209 feet long with a wingspan of 199 feet, weighs between 506,000 and 535,000 pounds, and is capable of carrying 375 passengers on flights up to 4,630 nautical miles.

A second version of the 777 will carry 305 passengers and fly 7,230 nautical miles in the three-class configuration preferred for long intercontinental routes. Other members of the envisioned family will carry up to 550 passengers or fly farther than today's 747-400.

The 777 was the first "digitally designed" aircraft—it was literally a paperless design process. The 777 was created by cross-functional teams and produced using advanced manu-facturing techniques. Boeing took the unusual step of involving customers from the onset of the project. In addition to United Airlines, Cathay Pacific, Japan, and Nippon Airlines were involved as advisors to the design teams.

Company History

The Boeing Company has been building airplanes since 1916. The company is organized into three major business segments: Commercial Airplane Group, Defense & Space Group, and Information & Support Services. About 80 percent of Boeing's business comes from commercial customers and 20 percent from U.S. government contracts. Sales for the year ended December 31, 1996 were $22.7 billion, with net earnings of $1,095 million. Boeing (including its subsidiaries) employs about 110,000 people—with most of its major operations located in the Seattle/Puget Sound area of Washington state.

New Product Design Process

Like most other companies in the past, Boeing designed its products following a fairly traditional process. Individual departments completed their part of the project and passed on drawings and other documentation to the next department, often with little communication between groups. The last activity was the creation of the maintenance manual. Mechanics were not involved and had to wait until the design was complete and the engineers wrote the document. They delivered the maintenance manual to the airlines after the aircraft had been delivered.

The design of the 777 represented a shift for everyone, including Boeing's customers. Customer advisors provided more than a thousand suggestions to Boeing designers, ranging from the width and configuration of the aircraft to reliability, maintenance, and operational considerations (Tapscott, 1996).

The cross-functional design teams consisted of engineering, procurement, manufacturing, operations, customer service, sales, and marketing. Mechanics were involved throughout the design process. The teams were organized around elements of the aircraft rather than according to function, as had been done in the past.

The engineers used sophisticated tools on computer work-stations to design the plane. The Boeing 777 was built first as a virtual airplane, existing only on a computer program called FlyThru. The 777 aircraft did not need a physical mockup because the design technology allowed designers to check spacing and clearances accurately. Engineers were able to work together because they had simultaneous access to the design. Distance ceased to be an impediment because the teams were able to collaborate on the same three-dimensional design, regardless of the locations of their members.

Sophisticated computer-aided, three-dimensional interactive design and finite analysis tools, developed by Dassault Systems of France and licensed in the United States through IBM, were used to create a digitized model of the aircraft. The model allowed manufacturing to ensure that parts would fit and mechanics to determine if a human could physically enter an area to carry out repairs. Boeing estimated that a paper-based design would take 30 to 40 percent longer to complete.

Production information and updates on the status of the aircraft were made available to more than 500 suppliers around the world. Thus the design of the 777 went full circle, from customers to all of the design teams to Boeing's suppliers. All parties were able to work together and collaborate as needed. Information and individual/group know-how were available to all members of each team on a demand basis. This performance support solution is a remarkable achievement that gives Boeing an edge in a highly competitive marketplace.

This new design process yielded the following results:

❏ Knowledge was shared and problems were identified before parts were manufactured.

❏ Engineering changes at the early stages of production were reduced.

❏ Manufacturing costs were reduced because parts were integrated "digitally" before going to production.

❏ Scrap and rework of parts and designs were reduced by 60 to 90 percent compared to previous design processes.

The 777 development process represents a whole new way of building airplanes. With digital design, the parts are more accurate and easier to assemble, which results in less drag and fuel consumption. In spite of competition from the Airbus, the Boeing 777 has been able to secure 75 percent of the market.

Nortel (Northern Telecom)

Like many large successful companies, Nortel has a number of design centers around the world. As a consequence, the design expertise needed for a particular project is likely to be resident at several different locations. In addition, Nortel often outsources various elements of the design to outside suppliers. The company takes advantage of its private network infrastructure and the collaborative tools it acquires from various suppliers to establish information sharing and conferencing capabilities to negate the downside of geographic separation.

Company History

Nortel is a leading global provider of communications solutions, with 1996 consolidated revenues of $12.85 billion. Nortel designs, manufactures, and supplies complete product portfolios for wireless networks, switching networks, enterprise networks, and broadband networks for information, entertainment, and communications applications. The company has approximately 67,000 employees worldwide.

Nortel Techologies, the organization that designs products for its parent company, has research and development facilities in Research Triangle Park, North Carolina; Ottawa and

Toronto, Ontario; Richardson, Texas; Santa Clara, California; Maidenhead, England; and other locations.

New Product Development

Nortel investigated several groupware tools and selected TeamConference, in part because it allowed the company to initiate and receive shared sessions from Hewlett-Packard, Sun Microsystems, and Silicon Graphics workstations and personal computers. TeamConference is a real-time, information-sharing tool for application and whiteboard conferencing between users in remote locations. Graphics or non-graphics data from applications such as CAD/CAM/CAE can be shared in one-on-one or multi-party sessions.

TeamConference is a menu-driven program that enables the conferencing of a single copy of any X-Windows-compliant application (graphics or CAD/CAE applications such as Professional CADAM®, AIX-CATIA®, ProEngineer®, I-DEAS® and AUTOCAD®) among multiple workstations, X-terminals, and X-enabled personal computers. Participants in both local and remote locations can view and interact with conferenced applications in real time and communicate concepts and ideas to any or all members of the conference.

TeamConference is being used by Nortel in various locations to share:

❏ Pro/Engineer mechanical design data with collocated team members. The articles include model and drawing documents of switch cabinets, enclosures, frames, shelves, modules, piece parts, wiring, and customer installation

❏ Electrical design data from work being done in UniCAD, VIEWlogic, and Cooper & Chyan for the design and layout of printed circuit boards

❏ Software code during the development, review, and test phases

❏ Problems with software tools from the users and internal help lines or remotely located tool experts

❏ Segments from software tool training courses

❏ Audio conference minutes

The ability to quickly share design information on-the-fly, on an interactive basis, has proven to be particularly important in the conceptual and initial design phases of a project. Figure 6–2 illustrates how TeamConference can be used to share a printed circuit board design.

Design teams have real-time access to experts regardless of their location. Although there are no formal measures, the design teams are meeting or surpassing deadlines, and overall time to market and travel expenses have been reduced.

Traditionally, when design teams had problems, they would copy sections of mechanical drawings and fax them to one another. The receiving parties taped the pieces of the drawing together so they could collaborate with their col-

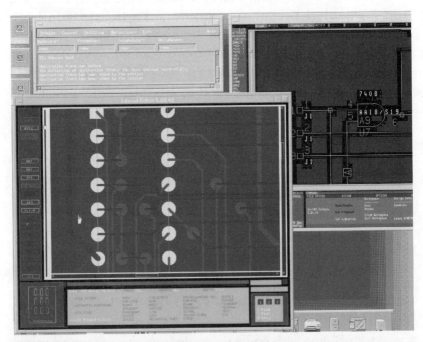

Figure 6–2. Team Conference enables two or more team members to review the same design in real time.

Source: Nortel Technologies, Research Triangle Park, NC

leagues. The process was cumbersome and took a long time. An electronic copy of the drawing could be shared only if both parties happened to have the same hardware and software platforms. Now the teams can share the drawings and make changes in real time since the parties are sharing the same information, data, and/or software code (Figure 6–3).

Software problems are easier to find and fix through a collaborative debugging process enabled by TeamConference. Developers at different locations can step the software code through its paces, observe how it is behaving, and find the faulty code in real time.

Nortel has a multiple-step process known as "Gate Reviews" that takes place at critical points in the product development process. Design teams use TeamConference to "walk through" the reviews in advance to ensure that requisite documentation is accurate and complete.

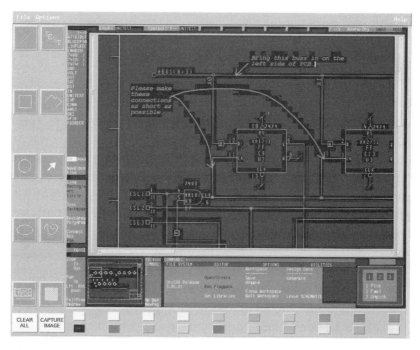

Figure 6 3. Nortel teams can share detailed design Information and make changes in real time.

Source: Nortel Technologies, Research Triangle Park, NC

As is the case for many large companies, Nortel outsources mechanical assemblies and other items to 40 different firms. Collaborative computing would shorten the time it takes to resolve problems when prototypes are being built. However, there are a number of obstacles to be overcome.

The network that interconnects the participants must have sufficient bandwidth to support real-time information sharing and whiteboard conferencing. Nortel has a robust internal network based on ATM technology that provides the bandwidth needed by internal users. However, many companies do not have the network infrastructure to support collaboration.

Companies like Nortel that implement intranets invariably deploy robust firewalls to protect corporate knowledge bases. Collaboration with third parties forces companies to breach their own firewalls. Since it is likely that companies will continue to outsource some portion of their product design efforts or collaborate with partners, it is important that vendors of firewall and collaborative software work together to find a solution.

The Olivetti Group

With 1995 revenues of more than 9,800 billion Lire, 30,000 employees, and a distribution network covering more than 90 countries around the world, the Olivetti Group is a major international player in the information and communications technology sector. The Olivetti organization consists of the parent company, "Olivetti S.p.A," and five operating units, each of which focuses on a specific core business.

- ❏ Olivetti Lexikon S.p.A focuses on the office products, printers, and office supplies market.
- ❏ Olivetti Personal Computers S.p.A is divided into two segments: the business segment, which addresses the needs of large corporations, public authorities, and business users; and the home segment, focused on private users and the family.

❏ Olivetti Systems and Services provides integrated solutions and services for large IT users.

❏ Olivetti Telemedia S.p.A provides telecommunication services, electronic publishing, EFT-POS systems, and interactive media technologies.

❏ Omnitel Pronto Italia S.p.A is Italy's first private GSM mobile telephony services provider.

Olivetti R&D employs more than 2,500 people in several laboratories in Italy and abroad. At the core of Olivetti R&D activities is Olivetti Ricerca (Olivetti Research)—a network of research laboratories and competence centers whose mission is to work closely with Olivetti's R&D organizations to develop new products, solutions, and services.

Creating a Virtual Laboratory

Olivetti Ricerca decided to introduce a new R&D model with redesigned processes and methodologies intended to foster more innovation and experimentation. Each of the labs had different mechanisms for sharing information, so it was difficult to leverage corporate know-how among the organizations. Because there was no central repository, researchers often looked for information that was in-house but difficult to find.

Olivetti set up a Netscape-based intranet that links all of the main Olivetti Ricerca sites and other labs in Italy and abroad. Employees use Netscape Navigator client software to access a wealth of information stored on an Olivetti multiprocessor system.

Researchers can find information about new technologies such as ATM, intelligent agents, Web developments, and interactive media applications. Each topic area contains articles, news information, biographies, and references to relevant Web sites.

Discussion areas allow researchers to debate, share experiences, project results, and collaborate to solve problems with commonly used software tools. Duplication of effort has been reduced since it is easy to determine if a problem has

already been solved by someone else. The "virtual labora-
tory" created on Olivetti's intranet enables researchers to
help their colleagues and encourages cooperation.
Productivity and creativity have increased.

In addition, the intranet is used to streamline processes
and improve communications. Project leaders are better
able to manage through access-to-project information such
as expenses, man-hours spent, and the status of procurement requests. Productivity has improved since project management overhead has been reduced.

Procurement of Olivetti products has been streamlined
since the entire product catalog is available on-line. The
company plans to develop a fully automated procurement
process that allows users to place orders and track status
through Netscape Navigator.[1]

The intranet has enabled Olivetti Ricerca to realize a fundamental knowledge management goal: critical information
is available wherever and whenever it is needed. The company plans to implement new applications that will help it
streamline internal processes.

Knowledge Production Processes

As this decade ends, more and more of what individuals buy,
sell, and do in corporations involves knowledge as raw material. The new economy is a knowledge economy based on the
application of know-how—to everything we produce and how
we produce it. Almost 60 percent of American workers are
knowledge workers, and eight out of ten new jobs are in the
information-intensive sectors of the economy (Tapscott, 1995).

Corporations that recognize the knowledge economy realize that information and knowledge must be delivered just-
in-time—in a fashion similar to that used to deliver parts to
automobile assembly lines in Japan and other countries.

Booz•Allen & Hamilton

It is not surprising that organizations such as Booz•Allen & Hamilton (BAH) have elected to develop Knowledge On-Line, a corporate knowledge system. Ernst & Young created a Center for Business Knowledge and KPMG Peat Marwick developed a Knowledge Manager. These "knowledge systems" capture and store the products of these large consulting firms. These performance solutions make it easy for consultants to access the best practices, the best thinking, and the know-how for all of the disciplines in the corporation. As long as an individual employee in the field has his or her notebook computer and access to a phone line, the intellectual property of the firm is available when needed. In effect, the knowledge system provides much of the "raw material" for the report production processes of the consulting organizations.

Company History

In 1914, Edwin Booz established one of the first management consultant firms in the United States. In the 1930s, James Allen and Carl Hamilton joined Booz. After becoming "the world's largest and most prestigious management consulting firm," according to *Time* magazine, the firm went public in 1970.

In 1976, the partners repurchased the stock and created a closely held corporation with a partnership culture, organized into decentralized regional offices. Each office "owned" its own clients and pursued its business independently of the others.

By 1989, it became apparent that the company needed a different structure that promoted cooperation across offices to match changes in clients' business environments. As Booz•Allen grew, it became more and more difficult to keep apprised of the experience and skills of individual consultants in the firm and to access the corporate knowledge base. Clients expected consultants to leverage the collective knowledge of the firm, so access to the firm's best thinking and resources became crucial. In addition, competition from other firms was changing the level of sophistication and specificity of the solutions required by clients.

The Knowledge Program

The Knowledge Program is a collective effort to capture, develop, transfer, and share the best intellectual capital available in all parts of the commercial business. The knowledge effort has two parts. The first part is content: the insights, client examples, industry and functional knowledge, and methodologies that collectively form the company's service offering. The second part is process: the infrastructure, systems, team structure, guidelines, and information needed to ensure that team members know what is available and have easy access to it.

Innovation Teams (12 to 15 members) interested in the same major topic areas work together to create marketable products. These products contain insights that apply across industries, address real business problems, and incorporate a set of best practices and methodologies.

The products of the Innovation Teams are High-Impact Products or HIPs. A second category was established for ideas that have good potential but are not as far along as the HIPs. This category is known as Special Interest Groups or SIGs.

The four HIPs that were selected are:

- ❏ *Performance Focused Management Systems*—key management processes and supporting tools, including information technology, which set appropriate objectives for short- and medium-term financial and operating performance

- ❏ *Business Process Reengineering*—a technique for revitalizing or transforming the enterprise by selecting and reengineering key processes

- ❑ *Global Care*—evaluates the overall value-added of the global core, including the role of the CEO and corporate overhead departments and recommends paradigm shifts that might increase the value
- ❑ *Customer Care*—builds customer loyalty, in terms of value and means, through channel strategy and management

The eight SIGs selected were:

- ❑ *Strategic Sourcing*—integrates both primary and secondary suppliers into the business with the intent of improving the purchasing process
- ❑ *Innovation*—improves the management of the product development process to stimulate growth and reduce costs
- ❑ *War Gaming*—uses tools that support clients in simulating competitive scenarios to improve and facilitate the decision-making process
- ❑ *Benchmarking*—provides a consistent definition and development of a database of qualitative benchmarks and overhead functions, and a consistent method for industry practices that develop benchmarks for value-added activities
- ❑ *Marketing*—enhances revenues and profits through improved pricing, promotion management, and brand management
- ❑ *Strategic Alliances*—practical framework of best practices based on a wide multi-industry database to help clients structure and support alliances
- ❑ *Change Management*—structures engagements and products to increase Booz•Allen's effectiveness in helping clients change and improve their performance

❏ *Business Unit Strategy*—a technique that incorporates
Booz•Allen's best practices in business unit strategy

Knowledge On-Line System

The Knowledge On-Line (KOL) system—a Web-based vehicle for collaboration and for establishing Booz•Allen's organizational memory—is becoming the company's future knowledge engine. KOL is an electronic database used to stimulate the exchange of ideas throughout the Worldwide Commercial Business. Booz•Allen staff have access to current information and know-how and to the experts who developed the ideas.

KOL was created to help staff members find the right level of information and/or the corresponding internal expert. The company elected to create a corporate intranet based on Netscape's client and server software and development tools. KOL is part of the Apple menu on PowerBook computers. By clicking on KOL, a staff member can choose from eight topic areas:

❏ WCB Knowledge

❏ Innovation Teams

❏ Training

❏ External Marketing

❏ Mailbox

❏ About KOL

❏ Q&A

❏ Booz•Allen Update-News

There are four key areas that are strategically important to Booz•Allen staff:

❏ *Knowledge Repository*—The repository contains more than 4000 documents that are cross-filed by topic, industry, and geography and by where the information originated and/or where it was applied. Conversational English queries are used to obtain a list of abstracts.

❑ *Expert Skills Directory*— The directory enables employees to verify skills and access information about Booz•Allen staff members' areas of expertise. The availability of this information on-line helps the firm to better serve its clients by enabling employees to quickly identify the right people to meet a clients' needs.

❑ KOL*aborate*—This application is a collaborative tool, based on Netscape News Server software, that allows two levels of collaboration: private communications for product development and client engagement teams to work together; and public communications as a virtual-knowledge help desk and for promoting new ideas through discussion groups.

❑ *Access to Legacy Systems*—The Booz•Allen intranet provides a gateway so that employees can access information from booking systems and from human resources and personnel information databases.

In addition, Booz•Allen consultants can access training-on-demand courseware, marketing systems, an employee directory, and a time reporting system. Booz•Allen plans to incorporate a Web-based digital library for external information on topics related to the firm's business. Further, it will incorporate live newsfeeds, enhanced collaboration and workflow capabilities, an executive information system, and interactive learning applications.

Knowledge is not included in KOL unless it is the firm's best thinking, packaged with complete context; it is reusable across practices/geographies; and it is fully sanitized. Individuals who want to contribute are given a template to ensure that the information captured is the most synthesized/mature knowledge of the firm.

KOL has been designed to suit the business processes in Booz•Allen. The information needed during the selling and consulting processes is available to all of the individuals who are working on a particular client.

The Knowledge Program and KOL are excellent examples of the application of information and know-how to the specific business processes of a corporation. Booz•Allen is being asked to share the value of its efforts with clients and prospective clients.

The following ROI analysis was prepared by Ian Campbell, director, Collaborative and Intranet Computing, International Data Corporation (IDC). The preliminary results of IDC's return-on-investment study of Netscape intranets found the typical ROI well over 1000 percent. The analysis was published in a report entitled "The Intranet: Slashing the Cost of Business." Excerpts are reprinted here with permission.

List of Benefits

The following quantifiable benefits can be used to justify the expenditures over a three-year period.

- ❑ Reduced time to find and access employee and collaborative information
- ❑ Reduced expenses for fax and telephone communications and overnight mail

In addition, there are several other benefits that resulted from the implementation of KOL that cannot easily be quantified.

Assignments for commercial clients are staffed with "virtual teams" composed of consultants from offices and practices all over the world. The teams are brought together based on their expertise. By researching each other's contributions to the knowledge program, they can come up to speed more quickly prior to meeting with clients.

KOL allows Booz•Allen to leverage its best thinking for its clients. In addition, the firm has doubled its publication output following the implementation of KOL.

Analytical Assumptions

❑ Tax rate assumed to be 50 percent for federal and state taxes

❑ Discount cash flow at discounted rate of 15 percent

❑ Straight-line depreciation over three years for hardware costs totalling more than $100,000

Analyzing the ROI

The return on investment is due in large part to the time saved by using the KOL system over the previous informal methods of information transfer. The intranet has allowed both newly hired and long-time consultants to share information and gather data to support decision making in a quick, cost-effective, and efficient manner.

To calculate the value, a cross-section of Booz•Allen consultants was surveyed to understand the amount of actual time saved by using KOL to share and retrieve knowledge. This average was then reduced by a correction factor to account for the inefficient transfer of time. To place a value on this time, the composite billing rate of an average Booz•Allen consultant was used as a fair indicator of the additional billable hours that were created by using KOL.

The financial worksheet shown in Table 6–2 is reprinted with permission from an IDC report entitled "The Intranet: Slashing the Cost of Business" prepared by Ian McDonald.

Booz•Allen has demonstrated that its intranet solution is a cost-effective medium for communicating, collaborating, and sharing knowledge between consultants in offices in 30 countries. With a three-year ROI of 1389 percent, the cost of developing the KOL system is quickly recovered.

Return-on-investment analysis of intranet solutions by IDC and others indicates higher rates of return than for other technology investments. Most corporations can quickly realize the advantages of ease of use and communication to any personal computer that supports a Web browser.

	Year			
Annual Savings	**Base**	**Year 1**	**Year 2**	**Year 3**
Personnel savings	$0	$6,969,600	$6,969,600	$6,969,600
Communications savings	$0	$130,000	$130,000	$130,000
Total savings per period	$0	$7,099,600	$7,099,600	$7,099,600
Depreciation Schedule	**Initial**	**Year 1**	**Year 2**	**Year 3**
Software	$61,818	$0	$0	$0
Network upgrades	$29,091	$0	$0	$0
Hardware	$218,182	$43,636	$43,636	$43,636
Total per period	$309,091	$43,636	$43,636	$43,636
Expensed Costs	**Initial**	**Year 1**	**Year 2**	**Year 3**
Maintenance	$0	$30,909	$30,909	$30,909
Personnel	$670,000	$783,636	$783,636	$783,636
Consulting	$30,000	$0	$0	$0
Training	$28,212	$29,212	$0	$0
Total per period	$729,212	$843,757	$814,545	$814,545
Net Cash Flows	**Initial**	**Year 1**	**Year 2**	**Year 3**
Total benefits	$7,099,600	$7,099,600	$7,099,600	
Less: total costs	$1,038,302	$843,757	$814,545	$814,545
Less: depreciation		$43,636	$43,636	$43,636
Net profit before tax	$1,038,302	$6,212,207	$6,241,418	$6,241,418
Net profit after tax	$519,151	$3,106,103	$3,120,709	$3,120,709
Add: depreciation		$43,636	$43,636	$43,636
Net cash flow after taxes	($519,151)	$3,149,740	$3,164,345	$3,164,345
Financial Analysis	**Results**	**Year 1**	**Year 2**	**Year 3**
Annual ROI		528%	988%	1389%
3-Year ROI	1389%			
3-Year IRR	605%			
3-Year NPV	$6,693,061			

IRR = Internal rate of return
NPV = Net present value

Table 6–2. Financial worksheet for Booz•Allen & Hamilton's KOL system   *Source: International Data Corporation, Framingham, MA*

Kaiser Permanente

Kaiser Permanente is a group-practice prepayment program that serves 6.6 million members in 11 operating regions. Medical and management personnel share responsibilities for organizing, financing, and delivering quality health care services to its members.

In 1993, the organization decided to collect and disseminate successful business and clinical improvements as a means for accelerating Kaiser Permanente's rate of quality improvement. Individuals had no easy way of sharing information or finding out what others were doing in other regions. As a result, there was a lot of duplication of effort. The first step undertaken by Kaiser Permanente was to compile and distribute projects and practices that exemplified excellent quality improvements. The system, which is called Learning Link, has grown to include a broad range of activities that help increase organizational learning, promote collaboration, and spread good ideas.

Learning Link

The Learning Link client/server environment provides employees with on-line access to e-mail, forums, classified ads, and an AppleSearch[2] database containing over 1,300 project abstracts. In addition, the AppleSearch database allows employees to access training and development courses and Kaiser Permanente publications.

As there was no effective way to train remote users, the solution had to be easy to use. New users receive a short set of instructions and a single diskette. No other training is required.

Cross-document, full-text search capabilities allow users to find information quickly using Boolean searches and virtually unlimited on-line text searches to Macintosh and PC users. Learning Link is used throughout the organization on an ongoing basis.

The entire system, including hardware and software, costs less than approximately $10,000. Although formal justification information is not available, the cost of the system has been paid for by savings from individual projects. For example, a region that was developing a women's health service saved two to three months' time and $8,000 because of the information available in the Learning Link database. In most instances, users indicate they save time and avoid research expenses because the information they need is readily available.

Although Learning Link is a relatively unsophisticated example of a collaborative environment, it graphically demonstrates the value of providing easy-to-use access to a knowledge base. It also shows that a small investment can generate a significant return.

Howrey & Simon

Howrey & Simon is a law firm specializing in litigation that is recognized for its work with F50 companies. The firm has offices in Los Angeles, California; Washington, D.C.; and Denver, Colorado; and employs approximately 750 people.

Background

Litigation attorneys live in a highly competitive, information-intense world, where cases can be won or lost due to the way ideas are presented in courtrooms. Matt Ghourdjian, national director of technology, advocated the value of using interactive media to express important concepts in entirely new and innovative ways. The firm needed a way to cull volumes of pertinent litigation information and to make it instantaneously accessible.

Over the years, the firm has successfully used video depositions in the courtroom rather than live witnesses or typed depositions. However, many attorneys felt the video deposition process was more trouble than it was worth. Attorneys often approached the day of the trial without having had an opportunity to view the video of the deposition. Production managers used a marked-up transcript to find the desired pieces of the deposition. The production manager needed to wade through hundreds of hours of video tape and master appropriate portions of the video tape to a laser disk.

Attorneys needed to lug a TV, VCR, or other cumbersome equipment into the courtroom in order to present the deposition. It was time-consuming and expensive, and attorneys were forced to rely on incomplete, selected views of the depositions.

In order to compete effectively today, attorneys need to be able to provide their services on a continuous basis for less money and to increase the quality of their services. Attorneys need access to all information concerning their case—at any time and anywhere. They need a more effective method for preparing and presenting depositions. In addition, the lawyers at Howrey & Simon need to complete the many hours of continued education that are mandatory.

Interactive Media Solutions

All members of the firm, including attorneys and secretaries, have networked Macintosh computers on their desktops. Howrey & Simon elected to standardize using CD-ROM technology as the standard information distribution and storage mechanism. CDs are used to deliver digitized video depositions to the desktop, continued education courses to attorneys, and software updates to all employees, as well as to archive crucial information. The firm presses its own CDs in-house.

Multiuser archival and retrieval system   Howrey & Simon deployed a Multiuser Archival and Retrieval System (MARS) to store all of its court cases and related documents. MARS is a document-imaging system capable of storing millions of documents and computer files on optical disk. Multiple users can retrieve documents by keyword or text searches and can view, copy, or print documents anywhere on the network. Howrey and Simon is leveraging its MARS system investment by archiving information on CDs, so that the paper originals can be stored off-site in less costly facilities.

CD-ROM-based depositions   The firm decided to digitize video depositions as two-hour movies and save them on CD-ROMs. A navigational tool based on AppleSearch and Hypercard enables attorneys to navigate efficiently using full-text, keyword searches through the entire deposition.

Attorneys are able to hand-pick appropriate portions of depositions to ensure accuracy and to create exacting arguments. Since attorneys create their own depositions, they are more likely to find opportunities that might otherwise be missed. Video depositions are more compelling than paper depositions, and CD-ROM technology transforms them into an economical, feasible litigation tool that is easy for attorneys to use in the courtroom.

The firm's current network is not robust enough to handle distribution of a sophisticated video library.

CD-ROM-based training   The firm produces its own training courses on CD-ROM incorporating text, graphics, animation, and QuickTime movies; they will be used for training the attorneys and clerical staff on company procedures and software applications.

The firm can produce higher-quality and more complete training using CD-ROM, since the medium allows them to repurpose exemplary presentations, cases, lectures, and other educational material. Each year, attorneys must complete many hours of continued education. In the state of California, 50 percent of continued education can be self-paced.

Ghourdjian notes that, "You can not imagine the sensitivity of the income-to-earnings ratio in a law firm. If we save five billable hours a month per associate by employing this means of training, the firm realizes a potential savings of millions of dollars in billable time each year, not to mention the savings in travel costs and hiring repeat lecturers."

Return on investment   Prior to the investments in Macintosh computers and CD-ROM technology, senior attorneys were able to work on 8 to 10 billable cases per day. Now these attorneys can bill against 14 to 15 cases per day. Howrey & Simon realized a productivity improvement of 28 to 47 percent.

AlliedSignal Aerospace

AlliedSignal Aerospace Company is a leader in the production of propulsion engines for business aviation and regional airlines, with emerging business across a broad front of new military and commercial applications. Two divisions— Equipment Systems and Garrett Auxiliary Power—have deployed an electronic work instruction system developed by Microengineering, Inc., of Las Vegas, Nevada.

Like other companies in competitive environments, AlliedSignal Aerospace looks for solutions that will enable it to build products more quickly, with improved quality, at lower cost.

AlliedSignal Aerospace Equipment Systems, located in Tempe, Arizona, manufactures aircraft components, missiles, submarine valves, and the propulsion system for the Mark 50 torpedo. Its manufacturing-operations assembly department employs 197 manufacturing engineers and assembly technicians.

AlliedSignal Aerospace Garrett Auxiliary Power Division, located in Phoenix, Arizona, builds auxiliary power engines for military and commercial aircraft. Building these large, complex engines demands strict quality control, testing, and attention to detail.

AlliedSignal Aerospace Equipment Systems

In early 1992, Equipment Systems decided to improve the process of creating and distributing work instructions for its assembly technicians. The company anticipated that it could reduce manufacturing cycle times and increase quality if it could find a cost-effective way to provide assembly technicians with clearer, more detailed instructions.

Traditionally, manufacturing engineers used computer-aided design (CAD) drawings and bills of materials to create tooling lists and assembly work instructions. The engineers used photocopiers to reproduce CAD blueprints, manually cut out the appropriate portions of the blueprints, and provided written instructions. The process was time-consuming and not completely satisfactory for assembly technicians. It took from two to three weeks to complete the documentation. Assembly technicians found it difficult to read and interpret the CAD drawings; they preferred to work with isometric drawings or actual pictures.

Interactive media assembly instructions   The Electronic Work Instruction team selected a Macintosh-based solution after analyzing proposals from several vendors. They decided to implement a client/server environment based on the A-PLAN Manufacturing Process Planning System from Microengineering, Inc. A-PLAN presents assembly work instructions in an interactive media format using a Hyper-Card interface. Each card can display multiple color images. Drawings created using Deneba's Canvas application can be displayed by A-PLAN.

A-PLAN includes an electronic bulletin board which allows assembly technicians to initiate on-line discussions with manufacturing engineers if they need help. Messages can be sent to individuals or groups.

The information that assembly technicians were accustomed to seeing in paper work instructions—tooling instructions, step-by-step instructions, assembly diagrams, inspection information, and bills of materials—is presented on-line, in color when applicable, and includes QuickTime movies and soundtracks (as shown in Figure 6–4). Interactive media assembly procedures convey the information needed by the assemblers more quickly and accurately than paper-based instructions.

An individual screen can consist of multiple windows, including a picture of an assembly, a QuickTime movie, a bill of materials, and assembly instructions. Clicking on the "Instructions" or the "Materials" window makes it the active window so the assembler can view all of the text in either window.

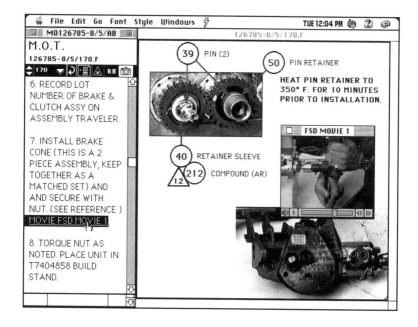

Figure 6–4. QuickTime movies demonstrate how to complete a complex step in the assembly of a brake cone.
Source: AlliedSignal Aerospace Equipment Systems, Tempe, AZ

Each assembly station consists of a Macintosh computer. Assembly technicians have access to assembly instructions that include text, sound, images, and QuickTime movies. They can click on "hot" buttons to view QuickTime movies or look at pictures. Color photographs enable technicians to quickly locate the components called for in the instructions. Assembly technicians can proceed with confidence since interactive media is more explicit than written descriptions or engineering drawings.

In addition to the video capability offered by QuickTime, it is also being used to compress images. Images, which can be 1 MB or more, are compressed by a factor of ten so they require less storage space and network bandwidth.

As shown in Figure 6–5, a window that presents special instructions is opened by clicking on the underlined text in NOTE 12. In this case, detailed information is provided about

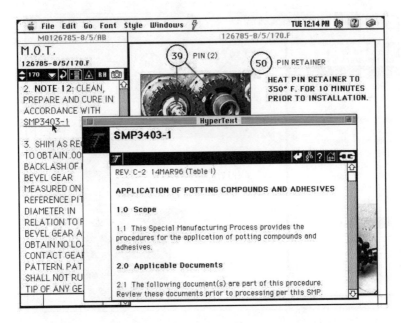

Figure 6–5. The hypertext capabilities of A-PLAN enable the assembly technician to review special manufacturing instructions.
Source: AlliedSignal Aerospace Equipment Systems, Tempe, AZ

a special manufacturing process that uses potting compounds and adhesives.

As shown in Figure 6–6, the documentation includes the part numbers for parts, the compounds, and the tools needed to assemble the motor assembly. The documentation process begins when the manufacturing engineers use a video camera to capture component assembly procedures. Both still photographs and video clips are selected from the video tape. The video is digitized and converted into Apple's QuickTime movie format. The photographs and video clips are put into a Hypercard document, which is part of an indexed Hypercard stack.

Still images are pasted into various drawings and annotated with part numbers and other labels. Video clips are used to illustrate complex procedures that would otherwise need detailed text descriptions. A 15-second video clip can

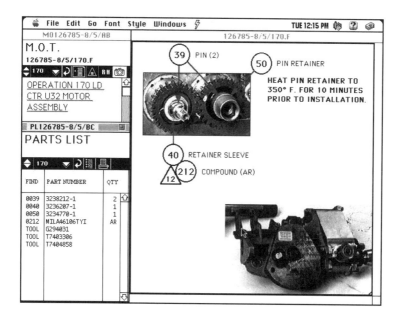

Figure 6–6. Paperless documentation provides all of the information needed by assembly technicians.

Source: AlliedSignal Aerospace Equipment Systems, Tempe, AZ

replace thousands of words and show the technician how to successfully complete delicate procedures.

Manufacturing engineers create interactive media work instructions on the Macintosh more quickly than they could on paper because the computer is linked to the other platforms used by design engineers. Thus they are able to access bills of materials on the IBM mainframe and CAD drawings on Sun SPARCstations. Manufacturing engineers are able to cut and paste CAD drawings using Deneba's Canvas application, add elements such as captions and arrows, then use the drawings in A-PLAN. The documentation process takes two to three days rather than two to three weeks.

Revised materials, text, diagrams, and QuickTime movies are stored on the file server. The application automatically accesses the most recent files and, if necessary, retrieves them from the network. Electronic updates provide better configuration control, eliminate the need for paper, and save time and money. As of June 1996, approximately 60 to 70 percent of the legacy work instructions were converted to interactive media format.

AlliedSignal Aerospace has realized a 15 percent productivity increase in the assembly area and a 15 percent decrease in the number of assembly-type rejects. In addition, the time to make changes electronically takes only 10 percent of the time it took to make the same changes using the paper-based system. An ROI analysis demonstrated a six-month payback of the cost of the project, which was $750,000.

AlliedSignal Garrett Auxiliary Power Division

The A-PLAN system was also selected by Garrett to ensure that mechanics had access to interactive media documentation while assembling auxiliary power engines for aircraft. The engines are much more complex than the components assembled by Equipment Systems and present some unique challenges.

The assembly instructions for everything but the fluid and electrical lines were based on the mechanical drawings made before the first engine was assembled. However, the best location for the wiring and tubing was not easy to specify until all other assembly was completed.

AlliedSignal Aerospace knew that customers would question the quality of the overall assembly if they received engines that did not look the same. The problem was aggravated because there was a 6- to 12-month time lag in completing the wiring and tubing documentation. Mechanics used temporary instructions based on 8-by-10-inch photographs and a parts list. However, there was no correlation between what the mechanics saw on the photographs and the parts list.

Garrett deploys networked Macintosh workstations at each assembly line and manufacturing location. The client server environment allows the mechanics to communicate directly with the manufacturing engineers. Further, the engineering workstations are integrated with the IBM mainframe and

Digital Equipment Corporation VAX computers used for manufacturing CAD/CAM applications. This enables the engineers to download drawings and Bill of Materials (BOM) information directly from the IBM mainframe.

The electronic documentation process is similar to that used by Equipment Systems. The assembly documentation includes images which can be annotated, on-line text, Quick-Time videos, BOM information, inspection information, build sheet information, and relevant calculations. The final result is an "information-rich" document that helps the manufacturing operation satisfy the goals established by the division.

QuickTime videos are used to show the mechanics how to successfully complete delicate procedures that would take a significant amount of text to describe.

The use of A-PLAN allowed the division to reduce the 6- to 12-month lag time to 2 to 3 weeks. The new documentation system reduced the time needed to assemble the auxiliary power engines and improved the quality of the work. Mechanics no longer face the ambiguity that comes from their attempts to interpret line drawings and parts lists.

In addition, Garrett found that the A-PLAN system reduced the amount of time needed to train and cross-train employees. The division was spending 10,000 hours per year on training and cross-training activities. The A-PLAN system enabled Garrett to reduce training time to 2,500 hours.

And finally, A-PLAN found valuable use in the division's troubleshooting facility. The department created a troubleshooting guide that combines the images included in the assembly documents with problems that have appeared during testing.

General Machinery

General Machinery is a division of Wheaton Industries, Inc., a diversified manufacturer and leading supplier of state-of-the-art glass and plastic containers for the pharmaceutical, cosmetic, scientific, and specialty care industries. Customers demand tolerances as tight as 1/5000th of an inch for their containers. General Machinery is a custom manufacturer of precision production equipment for its parent company and for the industrial and military markets.

With 120 employees, General Machinery is not large, but it is huge in terms of understanding how to exploit information technology and networked interactive media solutions to enhance its production process. The company has distinguished itself by the intelligent application of interactive media capabilities to its manufacturing process. Interactive media solutions are used in a factory floor performance system, and desktop videoconferencing with collaborative computing capabilities is used between departments.

When a worker needs to make a machine adjustment, plant floor personal computers display just-in-time, full-color images alongside the text instructions. Build procedures are documented by a foreman using a camcorder. The footage is captured and edited, and voice-over annotation is added using his or her personal computer.

Background

In 1990, General Machinery decided that it needed to reduce product development time if it were to remain competitive. It took 24 months to go from product concept to delivered machine. Jack Lowry, director of information technology, determined the importance of reducing the cycle time for all aspects of the business—from receipt of an order to customizing the product, from generating purchase orders for parts to building and shipping the product.

There was no formal, automated manufacturing system, and everything was done manually, on paper. Since the equipment produced by the company can contain up to 6,000 parts, a great deal of paper and photo albums were used to drive the assembly process. There was no single "expert" to consult who knew how the whole machine was to be assembled.

Workers spent a good deal of time looking for the information and parts they needed to adjust machines and build the equipment. Text-only instructions could be interpreted in different ways. Sometimes there were multiple copies of the same instructions because each person marked them up in different ways.

Neither the foremen nor the plant floor workers had any experience with computer technology when the transformation began.

Paperless Manufacturing

The company decided to exploit information technology and interactive media solutions to transform its business. The decision to go "digital" using IBM's Paperless Manufacturing Workplace has enabled General Machinery to document build procedures that included the exact assembly sequence of its products. The shift to a digital environment meant that information and know-how could be delivered in the most appropriate format (text and images, audio and video)—just-in-time.

As is the case whenever change is proposed, there was initial resistance to moving to computers. This opposition was overcome as employees understood the concept and recognized the benefits it would provide.

The Paperless Manufacturing Workplace consists of a suite of modular applications that allow for the creation, maintenance, distribution, and display of electronic work instructions using multiple media. The expertise of the company can be captured and made available throughout the build process.

Work-order modules containing video clips and images are prepared by mainstream employees using a high-quality consumer camcorder to capture the manufacturing process. The still images are fed into a paint program on a personal computer so text captions, arrows, and other visual aids can be added. The finished image can then be included in the build instruction sequence. Video clips with voice-overs can also be included to illustrate more complex steps.

The company is now able to provide step-by-step guidance based on the best information and knowledge in the company. This effort extends through the use of desktop videoconferencing with screen sharing and file sharing. This capability allows the worker to communicate first-hand with an expert to discuss a problem. All parties can see the same picture while they are talking.

Finally, workers no longer need to search for the parts they need because parts too are delivered when needed. The shift to a digital environment has allowed General Machinery to integrate information and to reduce the cycle time from 24 months to 10 months, with potential for more improvement.

Enhanced Customer Service

All production machines shipped since 1994 have included an IBM PC that acts as the operator interface. It includes Paperless and IBM's Person to Person (P2P) desktop video-conferencing software. The software helps the customer run and service the machine. The expertise of General Machinery is a simple phone call away since P2P allows company experts to see exactly what is happening on the screen of the customer's console. The company had an opportunity to improve customer service and to reduce the cost of providing it.

Epilogue

In spite of the early success enjoyed by General Machinery, other business factors forced Wheaton Industries to suspend the operation of the subsidiary and, with it, the Paperless Manufacturing System. The reduction in cycle time from 24 to 10 months was remarkable, and it appeared that further gains were possible. The investment by the company proved, once again, that just-in-time information and know-how have the potential to empower the workforce in a dramatic fashion. The overall result was a breakthrough—not simply an incremental improvement—and it became evident that the breakthrough was extendable to other business processes.

REFERENCES

Kalpakjian, Serope. 1992. *Manufacturing engineering and technology*. New York: Addison-Wesley Publishing Company.

Tapscott, Don. 1995. T*he digital economy*. New York: McGraw-Hill.

NOTES

[1] This success story is based on information provided by Netscape Communications.

[2] AppleSearch offers full text search and retrieval for accessing information stored on a server. Users can find information on topics they specify or let AppleSearch act as a personal agent that periodically provides updated information.

7

Interactive Media in Finance and Human Resources

This chapter covers both the finance and human resources processes. Neither provides notable examples of the use of interactive media, but each represents latent opportunities for its application. Professionals in both finance and human resources face the challenge of responding to the shifts that are taking place in their organizations. Business processes change as companies move to flatter organizations and self-managing teams. How should the finance and human resources processes change to better support the transformations taking place in other parts of their companies?

As I was unable to find any instances of the use of interactive media in the finance process, I can only suggest some areas that may be fruitful.

In human resources, many companies are taking advantage of computing and networking technologies to establish employee information centers based on kiosk and Internet technologies. Interactive media solutions allow employees to interact directly with company policies, benefits information, and personal employee data. They also allow management to leverage the same information to find ways to increase productivity and competitiveness.

In the section on human resources, I explore some areas that could be changed through the use of interactive media solutions.

Finance Processes

Table 7–1 lists the processes handled by corporate finance groups. Historically, finance was one of the first areas that took advantage of computer technology. However, it is not an area that has embraced interactive media.

Financial processes are dominated by numbers that are difficult to comprehend unless the reader is financially literate. There may be some good examples of the use of interactive media in financial processes, but with the single exception of interactive media annual reports, the research effort for this book did not reveal them.

On the Web, the home pages of most corporations provide access to annual reports. Typically the reports contain text, graphics, and photographic images. In some cases, CEO comment audio clips are included. The Web offers the

Asset management	Payables
Capital budgets	Receivables
Forecasting	Management reports
Inventory management	Tax reports
Lease management	Annual reports
Operating budgets	Treasury
Cost accounting	Cash management
Foreign exchange	Mergers and acquisitions

Table 7–1. Finance processes typical of large corporations

potential to provide a great deal of information that may be of interest to readers.

Audio and video clips could be added to introduce the viewer to the management team, to show the products in use by existing customers, and to provide a tour of some of the company's facilities. The annual report could provide a richer panoply of information about the company.

The "dis-organization" of traditional vertical structures by big corporations into small, independent, multidisciplinary units of 10, 20, 30, 40, or 50 individuals accompanies the need to turn workers into business people (Peters, 1992). The finance group has an opportunity to use computer and communications technologies and to digitize financial results into information that is much more meaningful to individuals who make up organizational teams.

As business people, we need access to financial information that demonstrates the health of our business and the impact of the changes we've made in our business processes. When revenues increase 10 percent and cost-of-goods sold increases 5 percent, what do these line items really mean to the members of a multidisciplinary team? How did the team's actions impact the corporation? What external forces changed the profitability of the business?

Current financial reporting is based on old operational business paradigms. With the impending end of hierarchical management structures, finance processes need to change to provide information to project-oriented teams in ways that match the speed and flexibility with which these teams are able to work. Will all team members be required to learn how to read a balance sheet and statements of income, when what they really need is information that helps them contribute in extraordinary ways to their part of the business?

Financials can be made more valuable to team members in two ways:

❑ By using animation, audio, and video clips in presentations of financial information

❏ By mining the available information so it is more directly related to efforts to enhance and transform business processes

In the first instance, imagine an animated presentation that shows how revenues are growing, month by month over the year, relating the impact of factors that changed the bottom line and proceeding to show what will happen if current trends continue. Video clips with expert input are included at pertinent points. These clips highlight the potential impact of a major change by a supplier or competitor or even by another team in the company. Teams could take advantage of desktop videoconferencing and collaborative tools to compare results and prepare new plans (Figure 7–1).

The marketing, sales, and customer service teams could have access to the early results of their implementation of a sales performance system that allows sales representatives to spend more time with customers. Based on experience to date, the team inputs new parameters. They instantly see the revenue and sales-expense projections based on several options. The team reviews plans for the next step in creating the infrastructure needed to support a marketing/sales/customer service knowledge base.

Using interactive media solutions, you can unleash the power of the valuable information already held in finance.

Figure 7–1. Desktop videoconferencing with collaborative computing enables teams to coordinate activities.
Source: Apple Computer, Cupertino, CA

Interactive media will put it in the context of the multidisciplinary teams that make up the "dis-organized" corporation.

Human Resources

Of all the challenges facing management, the biggest is the management of people resources. Companies must respond to regulatory and legislative mandates, the dynamic changes underway in their markets and in their organizational structures, and the need for increased productivity and cost containment—all at the same time. No one can meet these challenges without timely and accurate information. Human resources management systems (HRMS) exist to satisfy the company's need for timely and accurate information (Ceriello, 1991).

The term *human resources management systems* was coined by Vincent R. Ceriello in 1973. The term recognized that an effective system went beyond a computer and its data to encompass:

- ❏ System planning
- ❏ Properly selected and trained staff
- ❏ User support
- ❏ Policies and procedures
- ❏ Interfaces with other systems

At the time, it was an important distinction because it recognized the increasing complexity of the human resources process and the need for systems that encompassed many disparate components. To be fully functional, HRMS must consist of computer systems and the management process. It is more than a simple method of keeping records. HRMS includes master databases that make it practical to provide many types of analysis at reasonable cost and to support every functional area of human resources.

However, times are changing. Technological advances have enabled businesses to organize and operate in new ways that are more effective in global environments. For a growing number of companies, telecommuting is actively promoted as a means to increase productivity, reduce the costs of office space, and reduce employee turnover. Businesses are attempting to use technology to provide employee self-service for some human resources activities.

Many companies are moving away from vertical organizational structures to multidisplinary, self-managing teams. Our old notions of "climbing the corporate ladder" are no longer valid. There *is* no corporate ladder.

The turmoil associated with reengineering, downsizing, and "rightsizing" has created new relationships between employer and employee. Few employees harbor expectations about lifelong employment at a single company.

The human resources process must change to match the emerging needs of corporations and to take advantage of enabling technologies that can improve the ability of the corporation to manage people resources. It is critical that the role of human resources shifts from that of paper pushers to corporate resources who can help effect change.

HRMS needs to do far more than automate back-office human resources functions. The systems must be able to reflect the organizational changes that are affecting companies now, as well as those that will occur over the next decade. They need to be able to incorporate networked interactive media technologies as needed.

Human Resources Processes

The Human Resources or HR process in many organizations has been a bureaucratic, paper-based series of processes designed to manage and protect the personnel files of the employees of the corporation. When I was with large corporations, interaction with HR was always via forms for benefits, for hiring or laying people off, for performance reviews, for salary administration, and for other processes (see Table 7–2).

All of these processes generate paper that must be circulated to appropriate individuals for review and/or signature

Human resource recordkeeping	Succession planning
Benefits administration	Applicant tracking
Pensions administration	Position management
Salary administration/budgeting	Employee/labor relations
Employee health and safety	EEO/Affirmative Action
Workforce planning	Attendance management
Training administration	Absence tracking
Industry benchmarking	Performance evaluations
Conflict resolution	Incentive planning

Table 7–2. Human resources processes typical of large corporations

or processed in some other way before they are filed for future reference. Federal and state governments have fostered the paper nightmare through legislation designed to protect the rights of individuals and groups.

Document management, or imaging, has enabled HR to convert massive paper files to an electronic medium that can be accessed by keyword searches. Imaging invariably leads to changes in workflow and transaction processing and has been a catalyst for change.

The software industry has partially responded to the needs of HR by developing a number of human resources software systems based on client/server and workflow technology. These systems help automate the process and provide useful links to financial, manufacturing, and distribution applications.

For a number of years, interactive media have been exploited in self-paced training programs developed for employees. Certainly such training programs were capable of delivering all of the benefits that businesses have grown to expect from interactive media training programs.

Many companies view the human resources function as a non-strategic group. Efforts to automate some of its functions have been haphazard and, as a result, multiple independent systems were implemented. Quite often records were duplicated in different databases and it was difficult to share information. More recently, client/server and workflow technologies have been applied to integrate the various functions. Integration meant that different host-based databases and in-house-developed applications with master repositories could be accessed throughout the organization.

Realizing that many HR functions can be properly outsourced, companies such as Merck, a leading pharmaceutical manufacturer, developed a state-of-the-art human resources management system to support its internal downsizing effort. Information technology is being applied successfully to reduce costs and make access to human resources information much more successful. Such gains can be made regardless of the organizational structure of the corporation. In addition, these efforts consistently reduce the amount of paper needed throughout the process.

As discussed above, the vertical organizational structure that has been the norm since the dawn of the Industrial Revolution has shifted to a flatter structure, with increased emphasis on teamwork in core business processes. Every success story in this book is based on the successful delivery of the right information and knowledge in the right form, just-in-time, to the individual, as well as on the ability of individuals and groups to collaborate. The question is, "What are the human resources processes that synchronize with new organizational structures and core business processes?"

The enormous changes and dislocations that have occurred and continue to occur in the 1990s affect us all. In many cases, displaced workers are asked to leave their corporations and find new means of earning a living. Large-scale downsizing has spawned tremendous growth in outplacement firms. These firms' specific tasks are helping former employees work through their anger and frustration, take stock of themselves, and determine what the "ideal" job might be for them—and, finally, to successfully create a new position for themselves in another corporation or in their own business.

My own experience with outplacement was highly satisfactory. It provided an environment that allowed me to clearly define what I had done, what I did well, what I did poorly, whom I worked for at the time, and what turned me on. The insights of the counselors and fellow job seekers were invaluable. For the first time in my life, I was actually planning my new career rather than simply letting it happen.

This personal anecdote leads to an interesting question. Why wasn't this type of support and encouragement available to my peers and me when we were rising through the ranks of large corporations? Of course, it was my own responsibility, but why wasn't there a concerted effort to help employees grow and increase their value in the work environment? Perhaps it was just part of the old way of doing business, and it required a major dislocation—the movement from an industrial-based to a knowledge-based economy—to awaken all of us to the potential offered by employees.

I make no claims to being a human resources expert, but I do know that success, now and in the future, will be based on teams empowered through instant access to information and corporate know-how, working in organizations that know how to learn. Relatively new organizations such as PeopleSoft, Inc., believe that their people want to do a great job and accordingly provide all of the tools and support to enable them to succeed.

What is the role of the human resources department in the new, flatter, more horizontal organization composed of self-managing multidisciplinary teams? How does human resources contribute to the overall goals of the business? How does the company measure the value of human resources programs and their impact on the rest of the corporation? The rest of this chapter examines some of these opportunities.

Today's Horizontal Organizational Structure

In many organizations today, human resources personnel are being challenged by the emphasis on horizontal processes. In recent years, managers have noticed how horizontal processes which cut across divisional and departmental boundaries are important to the success of the corporation (Ghoshal and Bartlett, 1995). Efforts such as total quality management cut across organizations to instill quality in the company's products and services. Sales processes similarly involve almost every group in the company, and the collaborative efforts of these groups are important to the overall success of the sales force. Success in manufacturing also depends on the efforts of individuals from a variety of disciplines to collaborate on all aspects of product design, production, and implementation.

The research by Ghoshal and Bartlett, based on 20 companies in Japan, the United States, and Europe, revealed that business processes were more important than organizational structure to top management. When these managers looked at their companies, they saw processes rather than structure. The core organizational processes in these companies predominated over the vertical, authority-based processes of hierarchical structure.

These companies see and foster a process that produces creativity and entrepreneurship in front-line managers. They see and foster a second process that builds competence across the company's organizational boundaries. Finally, a third process is visible that promotes continuous renewal of the strategies and ideas driving the business. According to Ghoshal and Bartlett, these are the three core organizational processes that can exist in such a corporation: the entrepreneurial process, the competence-building process, and the renewal process.

Efforts by managers to establish and support these core organizational processes are important to the success of networked interactive media solutions in business because they recognize:

❑ The value of the individual

❑ The need to develop the overall competency of the organization

❑ The importance of converting data into information and information into knowledge

Companies that recognize the power of these three organizational processes are also likely to recognize that interactive media capabilities can help achieve corporate business imperatives.

Leading business book authors such as Peter Drucker, Charles Handy, Tom Peters, Don Tapscott, and others have recognized the need to dis-organize, transform, reinvent, or otherwise change current organizational structures. Tom Peters provides "prescriptions for success" in *Thriving on Chaos* that advise corporations to use self-managing teams as "the basic organizational building block." The size of the teams is restricted to 10 to 30 workers. Economic performance will increasingly depend on the quality, service, constant innovation/improvement, and enhanced flexibility/responsiveness that such teams can deliver (Peters, 1987).

Self-managing teams are responsible for all aspects of their part of the business. Each individual must be able to act as a business person who needs access to appropriate information, knowledge, and training. Consequently, the teams, supervisor-leaders, and managers need to be trained to do all of the tasks and activities needed to guarantee success. Engineers, technicians, shop floor workers, and others need to learn how to function effectively as team players. They must be able to budget, read and understand financial balance sheets, manage inventory, and maintain relationships with customers and suppliers.

Surveys indicate that nearly two-thirds of North American companies encourage employees to telecommute. According to Link Resources of New York, a group that tracks telecommuting and virtual-office trends, there are 7.6 million telecommuters. This number is expected to triple by the year 2000. As telecommuters represent a larger and larger share of the workforce, businesses need to consider the special needs of this group.

Telecommuters may require special support and training. Employee evaluation takes on new meaning when employees are working off-site. Evaluation must be based on work produced rather than hours in the office. Employees who spend most of their time in home offices may feel alienated and out of touch with the organization and its full-time workers.

New Roles for Human Resources

These organizational shifts portend an exciting new role for human resources groups. As a result, human resources will need to exploit all of the benefits of networked interactive media solutions to communicate, train, and support the efforts of self-managing teams. Human resources will need to function proactively and supportively to ensure that the teams have all the training, support, and access to information/knowledge necessary to ensure success.

Human resources groups are twice blessed as their corporations move from vertical organizational structures to project-oriented, multidisciplinary teams within horizontal structures. Not only do they have the corporate charter to look after the needs of the people-assets of the corporation, they also have tools in the form of self-paced training, just-in-time learning, and performance-support solutions. The normal functions of human resources, many of which are mandated by law, will continue, but an important new role will emerge.

Table 7–3 provides a view of the traditional and emerging roles of human resources professionals. I will use this table to launch a discussion of potential opportunities for the use of networked interactive media solutions in the "dis-organized" company. As an observer and analyst, I do not feel qualified to describe in detail the human resources process that will emerge. However, I can suggest several areas where networked interactive media solutions can make a significant difference.

Process Elements	Traditional	Emerging
Benefits	Paper-based system administered by HR	On-line access to files by employee
Retirement	Paper-based pension administration	Administered and planned by employee and spouse
Corporate policies	Paper-based document that is difficult to maintain and to use	Hypertext document that is easy to search by employees and easy to maintain by HR
Personal employee records	Paper-based documents administered by HR	Electronic documents updated and administered by employees
Career development	Hit and miss; often not a formal process	Help employees develop skill sets through self-paced training performance systems and lateral moves
Performance reviews	HR-directed process between employee and manager with some review by managers	Ongoing peer review process as part of self-managing team activity
Company bulletins	Paper documents	Access to current and archived documents with audio and video clips

Table 7–3. Traditional and emerging roles for human resources

Except for training, human resources has done little to embrace networked interactive media for any of its processes. Some organizations have established kiosks at various locations in their facilities which allow employees to investigate their benefits programs and to access appropriate human resources databases.

In other organizations, personal computers are being used to access human resources files. Employees can make changes to their own personal files, such as name or address changes; can make queries; and can achieve direct access to company bulletins. The technology empowers each employee to look after his or her best interests and relieves HR from several administrative tasks.

At USX in Pittsburgh, employees can explore their options for retirement using touch-screen kiosks linked to an IBM mainframe computer. The company offers a generous package of retirement benefits. Employees have many options to ensure that their retirement expectations are aligned with their projected retirement reality. After entering their personal identification number (PIN) and Social Security number, employees can develop complete retirement scenarios based on their personal savings, 401(k) plans, and anticipated Social Security payout benefits. They can take steps to adjust their savings plans to meet their retirement goals. When they are finished, employees can print the results for subsequent review with their families.

A new, more sophisticated human resources solution is being developed by the leading vendor of human resources software, PeopleSoft Inc. of Pleasanton, California, and IBM. The kiosks will be clients in a client/server network that allows employees to interact directly with all of the databases covering benefit programs, company training programs, etc.

However, there appears to be no concerted effort to apply networked interactive media to the more far-reaching opportunities associated with the transformation of the corporation. The trauma that results from reengineering, downsizing, and "dis-organization" is every bit as threatening and disorienting as was the shift from an agricultural to an industrial economy.

The consequence is a major dislocation that results in confusion, disassociation, and fear. It is also a major opportunity for human resources to exploit computer and communications technologies and digitized content in entirely new ways. Perhaps human resources professionals need to ask some of the following questions related to "dis-organized" companies:

❑ What does the human resources process look like in a "dis-organized" company?
❑ How do you recruit for self-managing teams?

❏ How should professional development be handled?

❏ What form of training or learning model is most appropriate?

❏ Does the compensation program need to be changed to recognize the unique nature of self-managing teams?

❏ How will career planning be handled?

❏ Should human resources professionals become part of the teams?

"Dis-organized" companies provide a distinct opportunity to recognize each individual as extraordinary. These individuals come with unique work experiences and ways of learning within an environment of changing work requirements and information needs. Human resources groups have a golden opportunity to re-invent themselves using networked interactive media solutions to serve the individuals and teams in their company.

Intranets can provide a tool that is relatively inexpensive and capable of handling on-line information storage, collaboration among employees, and transactions. With access to an intranet, all employees, including those who work at home, can have access to policies and procedures, their own records, and company news.

Desktop videoconferencing will add some expense, but it allows organizations to hold virtual meetings. When combined with collaborative tools, videoconferencing allows employees to work together effectively, regardless of location. Intranets can help integrate everyone in the organization, including telecommuters.

The requisite tools are available to respond to the changes companies are making. The question that remains is "How should the human resources process change to best meet the needs of the company and its employees?"

In the future, human resources professionals will operate at the factory, plant, and regional office level. These HR generalists will be much more proactive in the business itself. The pace of the HR process will become that of the group or team to which it is attached. These groups and teams will need to be supported by state-of-the-art HRMS that provide real-time access to information so they can respond without delay.

Once human resources has been integrated with the entire organization, human resources programs can be measured against overall business or process goals. Management will be able to benchmark HR's contribution to the overall success of the company.

Vince Ceriello, president of VRC Consulting in Los Altos, California, believes that employee self-service is the most significant shift that is taking place in the human resources environment. He also believes that many companies will outsource most HR processes by the turn of the century.

The head of human resources will be more of public relations professional than anything else, someone charged with the responsibility to ensure that the company is attractive to prospective employees. Another individual or group will be responsible for ensuring that the company complies with labor laws and government regulations. A third entity will be experts responsible for ensuring that HR information can be accessed in real time—information that is up-to-date and safe.

Line managers or team leaders will take responsibility for attendance, employee reviews, career planning, training, and other activities. In effect, some of the traditional human resources processes will be embedded in the day-to-day activities and tasks of managers and leaders.

REFERENCES

Ceriello, Vincent R. 1991. *Human resources management systems.* New York: Lexington Books: 6–12.

Ghoshal, Sumantra, and Bartlett, Christopher A. 1995. "Changing the role of top management: Beyond structure to processes." *Harvard Business Review.* January-February 1995: 88–9.

Peters, Tom. 1992. *Liberation management*. New York: Random House.

Peters, Tom. 1987. *Thriving on chaos: Handbook for a management revolution*. New York: HarperCollins: 356–65.

8

Summary and Conclusions

This book contains only a handful of success stories based on the implementation of networked interactive media solutions in business processes; hundreds more are available. Corporations are deploying networked interactive media through integrated performance support systems, just-in-time training, interactive services, sales automation, collaborative computing, and desktop videoconferencing. Interactive media are used to enhance business processes and to enable organizational learning systems to renew human capital.

The questions that remain after reviewing these successes are: "Why aren't more companies investing in networked interactive media? What prevents them from moving ahead with technologies that can lead to breakthroughs in performance? Why are they reluctant to follow the lead of other companies?"

Some companies seem to see the value from the onset and are willing to move ahead rapidly. For example, the aerospace industry is moving forward rapidly with collaborative design using collaborative computing and videoconferencing technologies. Other industries have yet to make significant investments in this area.

In the early 1980s, I had the opportunity to take a brand-new product concept to market—the Project Launch system (described in the preface of this book). Jim Hynes, formerly with Continental Insurance and now at Fidelity Investments, was able to envision the value of the system in the reinsurance industry after a few short conversations. Subsequently, we were able to prove that he was right based on a great deal of research and analysis.

Jim understood the reinsurance process and was able to see the potential benefits that could be derived from a description of the system and its capabilities. Most of us needed to see the results of our analysis of the process at Continental before we believed that the potential benefits could be realized.

My experience, and that of others who introduce new products in the marketplace, indicates that some companies do not have the know-how to determine the value in applying some new technologies to their business environment. Bridging the gaps between corporate management, information technology, and vendors could lead to a better understanding of the value of networked interactive media solutions.

The models and methodologies advanced in this book can help companies judge the worth of networked interactive media in their specific environments. Companies that develop a thorough understanding of their core business processes will have one of the keys to success. These companies will be able to prioritize the opportunities and pick the right one (or ones) based on its contribution to corporate goals.

These companies will also be able to determine the potential value of the technologies for specific tasks. Further, they will understand where and how and why value is realized so they can replicate success in other processes.

Finally, these companies will understand the demands that will be placed on their networking and computing infrastructures. For example, the implementation of collaborative design capabilities may require a more robust network infrastructure. However, there may be multiple applications that would benefit if the network were upgraded. Companies that understand all of their business processes will be able to rationalize infrastructure investments based on measurable benefits of several applications.

Each of the success stories in this book provides insights that could help you achieve success in some part of your business. In every single case, success hinged on just-in-time delivery of information and corporate know-how. Interactive media with the right level of media richness was used as appropriate to enhance the communication of the information and the transfer of the knowledge. When corporate goals and technology strategies were aligned, wonderful outcomes were achieved.

Unfortunately, no failures were reported. I say "unfortunately" because there is often more to be learned from failure than success. Most companies are not willing to discuss their failures. While few failures can be blamed on the failure of technology, many can be blamed on the failure of managers to develop a thorough understanding of business goals and processes and to align technology strategies with those goals and processes.

There is another component that is critical to success. In the end, human beings dictate success or failure by accepting and using or rejecting the technological solution. Accordingly, the individuals who are going to be directly involved—the major users—must be kept informed throughout the project. Management must earn their support, demonstrate commitment to the project, and ensure that training and support are commensurate with the needs of the individuals.

The fortunes of the automobile industry from 1981 to 1995 are chronicled by Paul Ingrassia and Joseph B. White in *Comeback*. The automobile industry in the United States, most notably General Motors, spent tens of billions of dollars on automation before it realized that robots and other technologies did not deliver the desired results (Ingrassia and White, 1994).

The big three—Chrysler, Ford, and General Motors—were able to create a new basis for long-term success only after they realized that the manufacturing process had to change, and that the change needed to be accepted by the United

Auto Workers and by all other employees. A formula for success in North America was revealed in 1983 when General Motors and Toyota established New United Motor Manufacturing Inc. (NUMI) in Fremont, California. Before recovering, however, each of the big three experienced near disaster. Their recovery was based on fundamental changes to the manufacturing process which enabled the companies to compete on a cost and quality basis.

Technology can and will continue to play a role, but the critical factors were the ability of Chrysler, Ford, and General Motors to change their processes and earn the support of union members and their management. Throwing dollars and technology at the problem did not produce useful results.

Analysis and review consistently reveal that the projects were successful because the individuals involved understood the business process in question. Further, by involving major users throughout the endeavor, project managers were able to make them feel that they were responsible for the success or failure of the system. In the final analysis, it had to be "their" system if it were to succeed.

The key steps to achieving success on a consistent basis are discussed below.

Begin at the Beginning

Technology is never the beginning—it is an enabler that lets us perform tasks and activities cheaper, faster, and better. Sometimes the tasks will remain the same, and other times they may be modified based on a better understanding of business processes. Begin by understanding where and when technology should be applied to enhance the outcomes of the process and to satisfy corporate goals and objectives. Establish measures throughout your projects so you learn from your successes and understand why some things did not work.

It is important to determine not only how well you succeeded but also why and where so the success can be replicated in other parts of the company. However, even successful projects should not be replicated without examining opportunities for change. What works best in one area may not be an ideal solution for another—particularly if the environment and goals are different.

If you're working with marketing, sales, and customer service, start with your customers and their buying processes. In manufacturing, start with a thorough grasp of your target markets. Ensure that you understand, first hand, the wants and needs of the customers that make up the market. In human resources and finance, begin by understanding the organizational and operational shifts that are taking place to develop new roles for your departments.

For example, if your company is shifting to self-managing teams, how is your role affected? What does the shift mean to traditional human resources and finance departments? The processes that evolved to serve the vertical, authority-based processes of hierarchical structure may not be appropriate for the horizontal business processes of flattened organizations.

Human resources and finance may need to reinvent themselves to better serve the new models for success. In any case, it is safe to say that success will be based on just-in-time delivery of information and knowledge to the appropriate individuals and teams.

The discussion that follows summarizes the keys steps for each of the core business processes covered in previous chapters of this book.

Distribution

As mentioned above, if you are working with marketing, sales, and customer service, start with your customers and their buying processes. Find out how their businesses and processes are changing and where they are likely to go. You may want to design your entire approach to intercept the market at some point in the future. This is not a time to design the future by looking at your wake.

At the end of each phase in the project, revisit your customers to ensure that you are being successful in their eyes. Remember that customer service excellence may be the only sustainable competitive advantage in the 1990s. Be prepared to make changes in response to new input.

To ensure that you can be responsive, it is critical that your overall design is flexible enough to accommodate change. Even though you may choose to implement only a small portion of your "grand design," it is critical that the grand design offer the flexibility for change.

Invest in a thorough understanding of the marketing, sales, and customer service processes so you can determine where just-in-time delivery of information and knowledge will enhance the process. Apply technology first to those tasks and activities that are deemed to be critical success factors. You may be able to achieve 80 percent of the result that you want by investing 20 percent of the amount needed for a total solution. The expense of realizing the last 20 percent may be more than you're willing to pay.

Use ROI analysis to determine the "art-of-the-possible" from a payback perspective, to gain the support of your management team, and to determine what worked and what did not.

As has been demonstrated, networked interactive media can have a significant impact on marketing, sales, and customer service. As we learned in the Acme advertising case study in Chapter 5, the payback in some parts of your business can be enormous.

Even if you do not intend to develop a single system for marketing, sales, and customer service, look for opportunities to integrate the three processes and ensure that your system design could accommodate all three in the future. It is unlikely that the pace of change is going to slow down, so you will want to leave your options open.

In an era where "putting the customer first" is the number one goal of many corporations, this may be the time to take advantage of networked interactive media—first in the customer service process and then in sales and marketing.

Although it is popular today to consider outsourcing customer service, such actions should be considered very carefully.

On the positive side, it is possible to reduce costs by outsourcing. You can use distributed database and collaborative computing technology to ensure that your experts can take over if the third party is unable to handle specific situations. In many cases, third parties do an admirable job.

If customer service excellence provides sustainable competitive advantage, why should it be turned over to a third party? If you need more information from your customer base, why take a chance by turning over this information channel to an outside organization? If a third party is positioned between you and your customers, will the information flow between you and your customer be impeded?

If customer service excellence is key to your future success, perhaps your overall objective should be to develop an integrated system that fully supports the information and knowledge needs of marketing and sales as well as customer service. An integrated system could include an outsourcing firm as long as you are satisfied that nothing gets lost in the translation between your customers and the third party.

Investments in marketing, sales, and customer service tend to yield excellent internal rates of return. All three groups are well paid, and all can have a significant impact on your bottom line if their productivity is improved. In addition, these groups can be the key to programs designed to "keep customers for life."

Intranets can be particularly valuable for ensuring that all of your field people have access to each other and to the information and know-how they need. The Web holds the specter of great promise, but it is in its infancy. Nonetheless, it is an opportunity to learn about the potential it offers to develop entirely new forms of relationships with customers. The Web may offer the best possible feedback mechanism if you are successful in getting the attention of your customers and soliciting feedback.

Finance

Finance is not being used to rally the workforce around corporate goals and objectives. Nor is it used to teach employees what is going on in the company or what is succeeding and what is failing.

Interactive media could enable companies to present financial information so that those of us who aren't "numbers" people can understand what is happening in our companies. It is hard to get excited about your company's success when the only manifestation of success is the bottom line of a spreadsheet. It's even more difficult to develop an appreciation of the role that you and your team played in the success of the company.

If you and your team continue along the same path, what impact will it have on revenue and profitability, on customer service and support, on product quality and time to market, and so on? Experts note that self-managing teams are the wave of the future and that team members make good business decisions when equipped with appropriate information and know-how. Why not use interactive media to make financial results "living, breathing entities" that respond to stimuli and change visibly over time?

Animated charts could be used for "what-if" games by team members to demonstrate a result that is meaningful to them in terms they can understand.

❏ What if our team were able to reduce the time to market by 20 percent?
The revenue stream would begin sooner and the product would generate more money.

❏ What if we could make our products more reliable?
Customers would place higher value on the products, and the company would realize significant savings in warranty costs.

❏ What if our group continues to increase revenues 15 percent per year in a market that is growing 20 percent per year?
The chart would show that market share diminishes to the point that you may no longer be a viable player in that market.

❏ What if I contribute another 2 percent of my gross
earnings to my 401(k) plan?
*The results would show how much more money you would have
for retirement and/or when you could retire with a specified
monthly income.*

Animated charts make financials real because the results
can be portrayed in more dramatic fashion. Further, individuals and teams can readily see the results of their planned
actions.

It is commonly accepted that American companies, in comparison to those in other countries, are driven by short-term
rather than long-term goals. The individuals and teams in
finance can make a significant new contribution to the well-
being of their fellow employees by using interactive media
to present the consequences of business actions in ways that
are compelling and dramatic.

Human Resources

Most industries recognize the importance of getting the best
out of individuals and teams in their organizations. But rather
than focusing on ways to accomplish this, human resources
has often operated as a bureaucracy in charge of the paper
nightmare associated with personnel files.

The first step seems to be clear: employee self-service
realized through kiosks, personal computers, and intranets
will free up human resources professionals to work more
closely with business management. The combination of
human resource management systems and networked interactive media heralds a new beginning for human resources.

The concepts of a learning organization, lifelong learning,
and just-in-time learning suggest that human resources could
play a new role directed toward employee renewal. If corporate success is predicated on the success of individual teams
and team members, then corporations should be planning
and implementing the systems that will enable them to learn
In fact, the teams need to learn *how* to learn. For example,
employees who learned to thrive in the vertical hierarchies

of the past need to learn how to thrive in the horizontal, process-oriented structures that represent the future. Human resources professionals are logical champions for this cause.

Although technologies enable us to do things we could not even consider a few years ago, human beings are ultimately responsible for making things work. Human resources professionals need to become more aware of the possibilities offered by technologies so they can understand the opportunities that will be presented.

As discussed in the context of the automobile industry, technology does not solve the problem. The question remains: How can human resources professionals prepare their organizations to take advantage of the technological breakthroughs that are just around the corner? Human resources needs to work with all groups to ensure that the organization is ready to utilize the breakthrough technologies that can make or break their company.

An interesting paradigm seems to be emerging. Technology will continue its inexorable advancement, but individual technologies cannot succeed unless the value of the technologies is understood and accepted in the context of business processes. Employees can achieve the breakthroughs in performance demanded by the global competitive environment only if they understand and accept technologies and the need for change—especially in good times.

Human resources professionals need to become the agents of change in their companies, helping to prepare employees for the changes that are inevitable. Only then will companies recognize the need for change and position themselves to get the best out of their investments in technology.

Manufacturing

In manufacturing, start with a thorough understanding of the markets you are trying to satisfy. What are the needs and wants of the customers and potential customers that make up each segment of your market? In this interactive digital age, quality and price continue to be important, but so is the ability to build products made to order. Manufacturing must be nimble, because product life cycles are short, and agile as a result of increased competition in global markets.

Many companies aren't building the products today that will be their largest source of revenue in one or two years. Networked interactive media can help reduce product design and development cycles. Companies can use collaborative design technologies to involve all the individuals and groups that can contribute to product design—including their customers.

Whether your products are tangible devices or information, the same principles apply. Once again, it is important to understand the process before attempting to apply technology. As we saw at General Machinery (see the case study in Chapter 6), the value of going to a paperless manufacturing system was accentuated by a decision to provide just-in-time learning, desktop videoconferencing, and collaborative computing.

AlliedSignal Aerospace used electronic assembly instructions to advantage in two manufacturing plants to improve product quality, shorten time to market, and reduce costs.

Nortel took advantage of collaborative design capabilities to reduce the time it takes to design products while taking advantage of corporate knowledge and the experience of its employees—regardless of where they are located.

At Booz•Allen & Hamilton, Price Waterhouse, and other large consulting firms, management has recognized that their best assets—corporate information, know-how, and best practices—were not fully leveraged until employees could access them.

In the final analysis, it doesn't matter if you are producing widgets or management reports. Delivery of information and know-how on a just-in-time basis is critical to the success of the operation.

The End Is the Beginning

A recently completed study by the Simon School of Business of the University of Rochester indicates that U.S. corporations, which have spent millions of dollars on information systems for their manufacturing operations, have not realized sufficient return on their investments. These corporations failed to develop a sustainable competitive advantage or acquire an effective competitive weapon.

The analysis focused on the adoption and business impact of computer-integrated manufacturing (CIM) and determined that it was being implemented by engineers and line managers rather than senior managers. As a result, CIM was focused on reducing costs and improving technology rather than corporate-wide integration of information systems.

The lack of business process integration across functional areas such as marketing, purchasing, and production planning, and across key technologies such as MRP, CAD, and robotics, is the major stumbling block in the implementation of CIM. Further, the study noted that managers focused on the "technological trees rather than the strategic forest."

The results of the study are consistent with the thesis of this book. It is critical that senior corporate managers understand their fundamental or core business processes. All of the "clues" needed to successfully apply technology are available in the understanding of the processes. Even though you may choose to implement a single system in the process, you should do so with an understanding of how the system will be integrated across other functional areas and with other technologies.

At the most fundamental level, the media-rich environments created by the application of networked interactive media simply enhance the communication of information and the transfer of knowledge or know-how. Senior business managers can combine this simplistic view with their understanding of corporate goals and objectives and core business processes to become more agile, more competitive, and more responsive in the global marketplace.

REFERENCE

Ingrassia, Paul, and White, Joseph B. 1994. *Comeback: The fall and rise of the American automobile industry.* New York: Simon and Schuster.

Index

A

A-PLAN Manufacturing Process
     Planning System, 224
Abbott Laboratories, 134, 141
accounts payable, 236
accounts receivable, 236
Acme case study, 159–169
advertising, 140
advertising process, 148–158
Aim 21/Brand Driver, 155, 160–169
AlliedSignal Aerospace, 193,
     223–229, 263
AltaVista Internet search engine, 50
annual reports, 236
AnyLAN, 12
Apple Computer, 11, 21, 41, 50, 55,
     64, 69, 72, 118, 169–179
Apple Reference, Performance,
     and Learning Expert sys-
     tem. See ARPLE
Apple Service Source, 50, 72–81
AppleSearch, 222, 233
application types, 66
architects, applications for, 36
ARPLE, 41, 50, 169–179
Aspen Institute, 17
assembly work instructions,
     223–224
asset management, 236
Asynchronous Transfer Mode
     (ATM) technology, 12, 14, 58
AT&T, 146

audience-centric advertising, 157
authoring tools, 64
automobile industry, 108, 255
Avery Dennison, 157

B

Ball, Stephen, 90
Banc One Corporation, 43
Bandag, Inc., 32–33
bandwidth, 12
Barlett, Christopher A., 6, 17, 244,
     250
Bear Stearns & Co, 50–51
benefits
     Acme Brand Driver, 166
     Apple Service Source CD, 77
     determining, 112–114
     quantifiable, 112
benefits administration, 241
Bergen Brunswig, 108
beta tests, 197
Boeing Aircraft, 21, 201–204
bookmarks, 84
Booz•Allen & Hamilton, 21, 27,
     194, 211–218, 263
Boulton, David, 56
broadband networking technolo-
     gies, 13, 58
broadcast television advertising,
     148
builder applications, 36
Builder magazine, 36

3-4 days   go over the findings ?

2 types ① Heuristic → professional assessment   in the
                    not every user issue   ↳ how you fix

② Recruit users that meet their requirements →
              a screener → recruiter would go out and
                    find people that
                6+ couple of backups

@ Lab, in town place   2 days ½ in lab

couple of d
Typical scenarios →
PC
     start analysis, what was found
good set of user data
     7 days   to put recommendations
                $1,500 /day

Lab costs →
$75 /hour market research rates

Usibility Engineering Testing → go in with goals
↓